Islamic Laws of
Death and Burial

Islamic Laws of Death and Burial

According to the Rulings of
Grand Ayatullah Sayyid Ali al-Husseini al-Sistani

The most important Islamic rules related to the final moments before death, the ritual washing and shrouding of the dead, funeral prayer, burial, and more

◈ I.M.A.M.
IMAM MAHDI ASSOCIATION OF MARJAEYA

Imam Mahdi Association of Marjaeya, Dearborn,
MI 48124, www.imam-us.org
© 2020 by Imam Mahdi Association of Marjaeya
All rights reserved. Published 2020.
Printed in the United States of America

ISBN 978-0-9997877-5-5

No part of this publication may be reproduced without permission from I.M.A.M., except in cases of fair use. Brief quotations, especially for the purpose of propagating Islamic teachings, are allowed.

Contents

I.M.A.M.'s Foreword ix

Acknowledgment xiii

Introduction 1

1. **Before Death** 5
   Signs of Impending Death 5
      Several important points regarding the will 8
   Attending to the Dying as Death Approaches 9
      Obligatory (*wajib*) acts 9
      Recommended (*mustahabb*) acts 10
      Detestable (*makruh*) acts 12

2. **After Death** 13
   Who is the Guardian of the Deceased? 14
      Multiple heirs 15
      Absence of the guardian 16
      Appointing an executor (*wasi*) to undertake ritual
         washing and burial preparation 16
      Additional considerations 16
      Obligatory acts 17
      Recommended acts (*mustahabbat*) 18
      Detestable acts (*makruhat*) 18
   Five Obligatory Duties after Death 19
      1. Ritual washing (*ghusl*) 19
         What about a miscarried child? 19
         Conditions of washing (*ghusl*) 20
         Requirements for the person performing the wash . 21
         Same gender or mahram not available 23
         How to wash the deceased 24
         Recommended acts of washing 25

Contents

Detestable acts (makruhat) when washing the deceased 27
If lote tree leaves or camphor are not available 27
Method of performing tayammum 28
Complete sequence of washing 31
2. Application of camphor (tahnit) 33
   Person(s) responsible for camphorating costs 33
   Obligatory acts related to camphorating 34
   Cases in which camphorating is not mandatory 35
   Recommended acts (mustahabbat) during camphorating 35
   Detestable acts (makruhat) during camphorating.... 36
   Illustration of camphorating 36
3. Shrouding 37
   Method of shrouding 37
   The shrouding of the wife 37
   Providing the shroud of a relative 38
   Conditions of the shroud 39
   What if it is not possible to obtain a complete shroud? 40
   Permissibility to shroud the deceased when acceptable shrouds are unavailable 41
   Purifying the shroud 42
   Recommended acts related to shrouding (mustahabbat) 43
   General recommendations (mustahabbat) for the shroud 44
   Detestable acts related to shrouding 46
   Illustration of the obligatory pieces of the shroud ... 47
   Illustration of the recommended way of shrouding. 47
4. Funeral Prayer (salat al-mayyit) 48
   Conditions for the funeral prayer 49
   Rulings for a congregational funeral prayer 51
   What is not required in funeral prayer 53
   The etiquette of funeral prayer and recommended acts related to it 53
   Method of performing funeral prayer 54

vi

Contents

Rulings related to repeating the funeral prayer 58
Rulings related to a woman performing funeral prayer 59
Participating in funeral processions 59

5. Burial 63
Rulings related to the burial 63
Method of burial 64
Temporary holding prior to burial 64
Transferring the body of the deceased 64
Place of burial 66
About the sepulchre (*lahd*) 67
Recommendations for the person responsible for burial rites 68
Depth of the grave 69
The coffin 69
Recommendations for the condition of the corpse ... 69
Recommended two twigs 71
When the direction of the qiblah is uncertain 73
General detestable acts (*makruhat*) 73
Ruling on exhuming the grave 74
Ruling for burial at sea 76
Inculcating (*talqin*) 76

Washing after Touching a Corpse (*ghusl mass al-mayyit*) 81
Who is required to perform ritual washing for touching a corpse? 81
When a ritual wash is not obligatory 81
What is considered a touch that requires washing? 81
Ruling on touching a corpse that has undergone dry ablution (tayammum) in place of washing (ghusl) 82
Exception from ritual washing for touching a corpse 82
Ruling on touching a corpse before it becomes cold 82
Ruling on touching an isolated part of a corpse 82

Contents

Ruling on touching a corpse through a barrier 83
Touching the excretions of a corpse 83
Acts that are [still] permissible for a person who is required to perform a ritual wash for touching the corpse.. 83
Acts that are not permissible for a person who is required to perform a ritual wash for touching the corpse 84

3. After Burial...85
Recommended Acts Performed after Burial...........85
Mourning for the Dead...90

Conclusion 93

Appendix 1 95
The Islamic etiquette of offering condolences to those who lost their loved one according to Grand Ayatullah Sayyid al-Sistani's opinion..... 95

Appendix 2 98
New rulings regarding washing, shrouding, and burial of a deceased person in a situation that involves infectious diseases (e.g., Covid19)........ 98

Glossary 109

I.M.A.M.'s Foreword

This booklet is part of a series of abridged and precise practical jurisprudential rules that seek to provide guidance to Muslims living in the West. The content of this booklet and the others in the series uses simplified language that non-specialized readers of jurisprudential texts can easily understand. The series clarifies the most important issues of applied Islamic practice (i.e., Islamic laws) facing our youth who are living and growing up in the West and who have reached the age at which they are responsible for performing and fulfilling their religious duties. These Islamic laws are written in accordance with the edicts (*fatwas*) of the top religious authority of the Shia sect, His Eminence Grand Ayatullah Sayyid Ali Husseini al-Sistani (may God prolong his life). They are specifically derived from his books *Minhaj al-salihin* (منهاج الصالحين) and *Al-taliqah ala al-urwah al-wuthqa* (التعليقة على الوثقى العروة); information published on the official website; jurisprudential direction we receive from the office of His Eminence in the Holy City of Najaf, Iraq; and through regular correspondence with great scholars among his students, such as His Eminence Ayatullah Sayyid Murtadha al-Muhri, His Eminence Ayatullah Shaykh Ali Aldihneen, His Eminence Ayatullah Sayyid Moneer al-Khabbaz, and His Eminence Sayyid Muhsin al-Hashimi, may God protect them all.

I.M.A.M.'s Foreword

This booklet focuses on the Islamic laws that relate to the deceased, before, during, and after death. This includes relevant matters such as recommended and detestable acts that the family and loved ones of the deceased should be aware of when fulfilling final directives, especially if the deceased has designated an executor to carry them out. We highlight the laws of death and burial for several reasons, most importantly:

- The urgent need for a large number of believers spread out over North America and in remote areas to know the rules of the dead and burial, especially in places that do not have a religious scholar close by so that it is difficult to request one quickly to fulfill religious matters as required and expected.
- The requests of many brothers and sisters, who have committed themselves to providing services for deceased believers, for the knowledge they need to fulfill their duties and deal with commonly encountered issues, starting from the moments immediately preceding death (*ihtidhar*), and including ritual washing, burial and all other relevant matters.
- An attempt to raise awareness of practical jurisprudential matters among laypeople and not limit the knowledge to religious scholars and preachers, because death is inevitable for everyone wherever they are. Therefore, adequate comprehensive information for this purpose should be available.

I.M.A.M.'s Foreword

The contents of this booklet are as follows:

- Introduction—various instructions for the stage immediately preceding death (i.e., when the signs of death begin to appear)
- Obligation of ritual purification of the deceased—the method along with illustrations
- Shrouding the deceased—the method along with illustrations
- The place and method of burial
- Funeral prayer (*salat al-mayyit*), supplication (*dua*), and inculcation (*talqin*) of testimonies of faith
- After burial—various instructions for the stage after burial, the importance of performing good deeds for the dead, and visiting graves

We ask God Almighty to grant us continued success in accomplishing these goals and in ongoing production of religious works, and that He blesses them with perfection and pardons any deficiencies, errors, or omissions. We hope that our dear readers will provide us with comments, suggestions and constructive criticism that can contribute to the improvement of this work and the elimination of any mistakes. Acknowledging that humans are not immune from error and forgetfulness, we note that perfection is only for Almighty God and His purified chosen servants.

Sayyid M. B. Kashmiri
Jurist Representative

Acknowledgment

We would like to thank and extend our sincere appreciation to all employees and volunteers of this blessed organization who contributed to the preparation, processing, review, editing, and dissemination of this booklet. We particularly would like to thank the respected scholars for their time and effort in reviewing the contents of this booklet and making sure that it is consistent with the edicts of His Eminence Grand Ayatullah Sayyid al-Sistani, especially His Eminence Ayatullah Shaykh Ali al-Dihneen, may God protect him. We ask Almighty God to accept this work and make it a means for attaining nearness to Him and elevation on the ladder of our desired perfection.

I.M.A.M.

Introduction

In the name of Allah, the Beneficent, the Merciful

"Blessed is He in whose hands is the Kingdom and who has power over all things. It is He who has created death and life (destined them) to put you to the test and see which of you is most virtuous in your deeds. He is Majestic and All-forgiving."[1]

Islam is the complete and comprehensive religion of God, and as such, it has not left any matter related to human life unaddressed. Moreover, it provides the necessary teachings and guidance to ensure happiness in both this world and the hereafter. At the heart of this divine system is the transition from this temporary material life to the permanent and spiritual one in the next world. The Holy Quran sometimes refers to this transition as death (*mawt*) and sometimes as the "take-back" (*wafat*). Death signifies an end to the life of the physical body while wafat indicates a return of the soul to God, who describes mawt by stating, "Every soul will experience the agony of death"[2] and wafat by stating, "He told Jesus, 'I will save you from your enemies, raise you to Myself, keep you clean from the association with the unbelievers, and give superiority to your followers over the unbelievers until the Day of Judgment. On that

---

1. The Holy Quran 67:1–2. All Quranic quotes in this book are from the Muhammad Sarwar translation.
2. The Holy Quran 29:57.

day you will all return to Me and I shall resolve your dispute."[3]

Regardless, death is a fact that cannot be denied, and it is inevitable no matter how much a person tries to evade it. God reminds us that "The agony of death will reach the human being as a matter of all truth and he (the human being) will be told, 'This is what you had been trying to run away from.'"[4] and "(Muhammad), tell them, 'the death from which you run away will certainly approach you. Then you will be returned to the One who knows the unseen and the seen, and He will tell you what you have done."[5] Perhaps the most important reasons why a person tries to evade death or, at least, not heed its inevitability is a lack of understanding of its reality and being unprepared to meet God and face His accounting. God says, "When death approaches one of the unbelievers, he says, 'Lord, send me back again so that perhaps I shall act righteously for the rest of my life.'"[6] This represents a confession by the person that they have neglected their duty, either in terms of knowing their obligations or fulfilling them. The divine response is decisive, direct, and constant, "Although he says so, his wish will never come true. After death they will be behind a barrier until the day of their resurrection. After the trumpet sounds there will be no kindred relations nor any opportunity to ask about others or seek their assistance. If the side of one's good

---

3. The Holy Quran 3:55.
4. The Holy Quran 50:19.
5. The Holy Quran 62:8.
6. The Holy Quran 23:99–100.

deeds weigh heavier on a scale, he will have everlasting happiness, but if it weighs less, one will be lost forever in hell."[7]

Therefore, it is necessary for a rational person to be mindful of this inevitable truth when conducting their affairs in this world and those related to the hereafter. Hence, we must know the rulings of God Almighty in this regard, and strive to implement them in the best way to live happily in this life and in the hereafter. As is the case for a newborn, for whom Islam stipulates various rulings, recommendations, moral guidance, and observance of rights, there are many obligatory rulings, as well as a set of ethical instructions, rights, and etiquette for the deceased. A person should be acquainted with these important details, some of which are obligatory to learn. Detailed rulings that require the attention of the reader will be highlighted in this booklet, starting with the moments before death, a step-by-step description of the rules when it occurs, and the stages afterwards.

---

[7]. The Holy Quran 23:100–103.

Chapter 1

Before Death

Signs of Impending Death

God has made death inevitable for His servants. Therefore, if the signs of death appear and it looks as though the person is close to passing (for example, due to an incurable disease), they must hasten to do several things that include the following:

- Seeking forgiveness and repenting to God—A person should constantly seek forgiveness from Almighty God during their life, whether for neglecting an obligatory duty or committing an unlawful act. This should arise from a continuous feeling of sincere regret and a determination to avoid the sin thereafter. Moreover, seeking forgiveness and repentance should not be relegated to the moments before death, but rather it is obligatory every time a person commits a sin or falls short in performing a duty. It is reported that the Prophet of God (pbuh&hp) said, "God will accept the repentance of one who does so before they see [the angel of death]."[8]

---

8. Al-Kulayni, *Al-kafi*, vol. 2, p. 440.

- Writing a will—It is recommended that believers write a will even if they are not liable for the fulfillment of any [lapsed or missed] obligations to God or other people. However, it becomes obligatory to direct a will (even if verbally), when death is near and its signs begin to appear if fulfilling required obligations to God and the rights of people depend on it. Therefore, the soon-to-be deceased must designate a trusted person to fulfill their responsibilities after death.

  There are two forms of wills that are related to the types of lapsed obligations that need fulfilling. These are based on

  - the rights of God that include
    - duties of obligatory worship, such as making up missed prayers (*qada al-salat*), required fasts (*qada al-siam*), and the pilgrimage (*hajj*) that must be performed once in a lifetime for anyone who becomes capable of doing so;
    - religious dues that were due and not paid, such as *khums*, *zakat*, or lapsed expiations;[9] and
  - the rights of people that fall into three categories:
    - Debts, such as those from financial loans; unpaid full or partial dowry owed to a wife; wages that a person owes to

---

9. The respected reader should refer to the *Islamic Laws of Expiation* booklet, already published in this jurisprudential series.

an employee or a contractor; liability for damage done to other people's property, such as scratching their vehicle or breaking the windows of their house; the seizure of someone else's property that is not returned to its rightful owner; or due to the damage or neglect of someone else's property.
- Expiation or reparations, such as those for physically striking a student, a child, or any other person without just cause. This is in addition to personal damages that Islam requires to be paid or as might be adjudicated by an Islamic judge or religious authority.
  - Restitution of various forms of trusts, such as the belongings of others that the person is responsible for (e.g., a borrowed book), or any other item that has not been returned to its rightful owner or any agreed upon service that has not been fulfilled.

For all the above (debts, expiation, and trusts), the rightful owner must be satisfied, either by the return of the item or by compensation of the equivalent value if the possessions were damaged [or lost]. Or, it must be ensured that they are satisfied and have pardoned the deceased if the property is not returned or restituted for any reason. However, if the owners [or their inheritors] are unknown [or unreachable], disposition of the possessions falls under the authority of the Imam (p). In such a case (i.e., during the occultation period of the Imam [p]), a person must give the possession or its equivalent to the poor as charity (*sadaqah*) on behalf of its rightful owner after getting permission from the religious authority (i.e., the qualified jurist or marja) based on obligatory precaution.[10] If the person is unable to fulfill what was entrusted and return the possession to its rightful owner, then they must direct in a will that it be paid (restituted) from the estate [of the deceased] and prior to distributing the inheritance to the heirs.

Several important points regarding the will

The following are points that one should be aware of regarding the will:

- The person should appoint an executor and direct the fulfillment of all their important affairs that need to be discharged after death.
- A will cannot be implemented beyond one-third of the estate. The other two-thirds is the inheritance and the testator cannot bequeath it to some of their children and deprive the rest. However, they are permitted to give whatever they wish to whomever during their lifetime. Fulfillment of any directives that exceed the one-third of the estate requires consent of the heirs.
- If the testator is afflicted with a mental illness such that they cannot comprehend and remember (e.g., Alzheimer's disease), then the will is not carried out and all their assets and possessions are frozen. In such a case, no one

---

10. Obligatory precaution (*ihtiyat wajib*) is an edict that means the follower may either act on this precaution or act on the fatwa of the second most knowledgeable current jurist.

is authorized to act upon the assets or possessions without the permission of the religious authority (i.e., the qualified jurist who meets the conditions of emulation).

- In some instances, people register their possessions or save their money in a bank account under the name of one of their heirs or some other person for legal purposes as stipulated by the country in which they live.[11] In such a case, it is not permissible for the beneficiary or person under whose name the property or bank account is registered to use or dispose of the property or funds unless there is a legitimate will by the testator allowing them to do so, authentic evidence of that fact, or by consent of all the heirs.

Attending to the Dying as Death Approaches

When the signs of death appear in a believer, such as rapid breathing, a change in facial color, and sounds (i.e., death rattle) heard from the area of the chest, the following rulings must be observed:

Obligatory (*wajib*) acts

- Based on obligatory precaution, the dying person must be laid on their back with their

---

11. Some countries do not allow a non-citizen or legal resident to purchase real estate under their name or open a bank account unless they become a citizen or obtain official residence status, so the individual in this case registers their property in someone else's name who is allowed by law to own property or open a bank account.

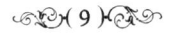

legs pointing towards the direction of the qiblah such that if they sit up, they will be facing it.[12]
- Based on obligatory precaution, permission must be taken from the dying person or their guardian (*wali*).

Recommended (*mustahabb*) acts

- If the throes of death become severe (i.e., dying becomes painful), it is recommended to move the dying person to the place where they used to perform their daily prayers, if it does not cause them further pain.
- It is recommended to reindoctrinate (talqin) the dying person with the testimonies of faith that is to bear witness that there is no god but Allah, and Muhammad is His messenger, as well to reaffirm faith in the twelve Imams and the fundamental pillars of faith, and for the dying person to repeat them.[13]
- It is recommended to reaffirm to the dying person the words of deliverance (*kalimat al-faraj*): There is no god but Allah, the Wise, the Generous;
There is no god but Allah, the High, the Great.

---

12. It is obligatory for Muslims to direct the dying person toward the qiblah if they are a Muslim and regardless of their sect.

13. The acknowledgment of the twelve infallible Imams (pbut) and the rest of the pillars of faith should be repeated to the dying person in a way that they understand so they can repeat them after.

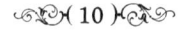

Before Death

"لا إلهَ إلّا اللهُ الحكيمُ الكريمُ، لا إلهَ إلّا اللهُ العَلِيُّ العَظيمُ، سُبحانَ اللهِ رَبِّ السَّماواتِ السَّبعِ ورَبِّ الأَرَضينَ السَّبعِ وَما فيهِنَّ وَما تَحتَهُنَّ وَرَبِّ العَرشِ العَظيمِ وَالحمدُ للهِ رَبِّ العَالمين"

NOTE: Based on a recommended precaution, the dying person should lie down towards the qiblah themselves if they are capable.

It is narrated by Zurara that Imam Muhammad al-Baqir (p) said, "if you encounter a person while they are dying, reindoctrinate them with the words of deliverance (kalimat al-faraj) which are:

There is no God but Allah, the Most Wise, the Most Generous, there is no god but Allah, the Most High, the Most Mighty. All praise be to Allah, the Lord of the seven heavens and the Lord of the seven earths, and whatever is in them and whatever is under them and the Lord of the Great Throne. And all praise be to Allah, the Lord of the Universe."[14]

It is also recommended to recite Surat Ya Sin (chapter 36), Surat al-Saffat (chapter 37), Ayat al-Kursi (verses 255–257 of chapter 2, Surat al-Baqarah), and any recitation from the Holy Quran to ease their death.

---

14. Al-Kulayni, *Al-kafi*, vol.3, p.122.

Detestable (*makruh*) acts

- A dying person should not be attended by a junub[15] or a menstruating woman.
- One should refrain from touching the person close to death; in fact, one must refrain from doing so based on a recommended precaution.[16]

---

15. Junub means someone in the state of ritual impurity because of ejaculation or sexual intercourse (*janabah*).

16. The term recommended precaution refers to a precautionary act that can be abandoned by a person because it is only recommended.

Chapter 2

After Death

Just as Islam has prescribed a complete code of life for human beings, it has also provided specific guidance on the aspects of human existence that transfer to the next world after the death of the physical body. Moreover, Islam considers the dead body of a human being to be inviolable, and thus, its sanctity should be preserved just as when the person was alive. It is narrated in the traditions that "The sanctity of a believer in death is the same as in life,"[17] and that Imam al-Sadiq (p) said, "The believer's sanctity is greater than that of the Kabah."[18]

Hence, the forthcoming rulings that describe the preparation of the dead, the ritual washing of the body, burial, and execution of the deceased's affairs are obligatory for the guardian of the deceased. Therefore, the guardian must fulfill these requirements directly himself or by hiring or giving permission to another person to do so. If he refrains from performing his duties, his permission or authorization is not required to carry them out, such that the obligation is lifted from him and all others if someone else fulfills the required acts. This is because it is an essential

---

17. Shaykh al-Tusi, *Tahthib al-ahkam*, vol. 1, p. 419.
18. Shaykh al-Saduq, *Al-khisal*, p.27.

obligation (*wajib ayni*) of the guardian and only obligatory upon others (*wajib kifai*) if no one else fulfills the requirements.

Who is the Guardian of the Deceased?

The guardian of a wife is her husband, who takes precedence over her father and son. For anyone other than a wife, their guardian is the heir who is the antecedent in inheritance based on the following order:

- The first group: parents and children
- The second group: grandparents and siblings
- The third group: uncles and parental uncles[19]

Q: What if the deceased has no heirs?
A: If the deceased has no heir, the Imam (p) is his inheritor, and [during his occultation] based on recommended precaution one must obtain permission from the qualified jurist or marja (the religious authority) to prepare the body for burial. However, if obtaining permission from the jurist is not possible, then permission must be sought from believers who are just (*adil*).

---

19. Although there are male and female family members in this group, there is a hierarchy of who should be the guardian of the deceased. For further details, refer to Ayatullah Sayyid al-Sistani's *Islamic Laws, Third Edition*.

Multiple heirs

When there are multiple heirs, males take precedence over females[20] in each group. If the heirs are of the same gender, it is problematic to give precedence to one of them over the other. For example, if the heirs of the deceased are their father and son, or [in their absence] grandfather and brother, giving precedence to one of them over the other is problematic, thus obligatory precaution must be taken in this case. The precaution requires that permission be taken from the one whose precedence is probable in the matter of guardianship. For example, if the deceased is survived by sons and a father, the obligatory precaution is to take permission from the father and not rely solely on permission from the sons. In addition, the permission of a brother does not take precedence over the permission of the grandfather (if he is alive); similarly the permission of a half-brother does not take precedence if there is a full brother of the deceased; nor the permission of a half-brother from the mother over half-brothers from the father; nor the permission of the maternal uncle over the paternal uncle. In such cases permission should be taken from both parties.

A minor who has not reached the age of religious obligation cannot act as a guardian for a deceased person. Similarly, someone who is absent and cannot be reached to undertake the affairs of the deceased,

---

20. The precedence of males over females in this matter relates to the issue of guardianship, which is a responsibility assigned to some males by Islam within its system of rights and duties. This should not be misunderstood as favoring males and discriminating against females.

either themselves or by appointing an agent, does not have guardianship of the deceased.

Absence of the guardian

If the guardian is absent and unreachable, it is incumbent on the rest of the believers to prepare the deceased based on *al-wujub al-kifai*, meaning that if some of the believers fulfill this obligation, it is lifted from the rest. However, if it is not fulfilled, the whole community of believers who knew about the obligation has committed a sin.

Appointing an executor (*wasi*) to undertake ritual washing and burial preparation

If a person appoints an executor to undertake their affairs after death, that person is not obligated to accept the responsibility. However, if they accept, they will not need the permission of the guardian to fulfill the necessary rituals. If an individual entrusts a specific person to carry out the preparation of their body after death, the latter must accept based on obligatory precaution if accepting does not impose any hardship on them [the executor]. However, there is no problem if the executor withdraws from this responsibility during the life of the testator, and the testator can appoint a different executor. If the appointed person accepts the task of executor, they take precedence in undertaking the preparation of the deceased [testator].

Additional considerations

Some additional considerations to know in preparation of the deceased are as follows:

- It is recommended to hasten preparation of the deceased and quickly fulfill what is required.
- It is necessary to ensure the sanctity of the deceased and not keep them in any place that infringes on it, such as places that are impure, places that are used for unlawful acts (e.g., bars or casinos), or areas of garbage disposal.
- It is detestable (makruh) to display the body of the deceased for viewing.[21]

Specific procedures must be carried out on the body after death is verified, such that it is known that the soul (*ruh*) has left. Some of these procedures are obligatory and some are recommended.

Obligatory acts

When death occurs, specific duties are obligatory for the guardian,[22] and if they cannot fulfill them [for any reason], those who know of the situation are obliged to carry out the duties based on al-wujub al-kifai, meaning that if some of the believers fulfill this obligation, it is lifted from the rest of them. However, if it is not fulfilled, the whole community of believers who knew about the

---

21. It is detestable (makruh) to beautify the deceased such as by cutting their hair and putting on cosmetics. It is also detestable (makruh) to expose them for the purposes of viewing by others. This may become unlawful (*haram*) if it is considered to be imitating others who display the body for days as a salute, formalized viewing, or to bid farewell, even if the body is kept in refrigerators that preserve it from disintegrating.

22. The one who is obliged to take on such duties was identified previously under the section "Who is the guardian of the deceased?"

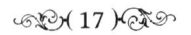

obligation has committed a sin. These obligatory acts are as follows:

1. Washing the body (*ghusl*)
2. Camphorating the body (*tahnit*)
3. Shrouding the body (*takfin*)
4. Performing the funeral prayer (salat al-mayyit)
5. Burial (*dafn*)

Recommended acts (*mustahabbat*)

It is recommended to perform the following things prior to washing the deceased, given that it is of benefit to them:

- Closing the eyes
- Closing the mouth so the lips are together
- Contracting the jaw (i.e., so it is not slack)
- Stretching the arms along the sides and straightening the legs
- Spreading cloth over the body
- Reciting the Quran near the deceased
- Illuminating the place if the person died at night
- Informing the believers of the person's death so they can attend their funeral
- Hastening preparation of the body for burial by not delaying it from night to the following day or from day to night time

Detestable acts (*makruhat*)

The following things are detestable before washing the body because they entail discomfort to the deceased:

- Leaving the body unattended
- Placing a heavy object on the stomach

- Speaking more than necessary in the deceased's presence
- Weeping by the deceased
- Leaving women alone with the deceased

Five Obligatory Duties after Death

1. Ritual washing (ghusl)

It is obligatory to perform a ritual washing (ghusl) on every person who is considered a Muslim, including

- non-Shia or non-Twelver Shia Muslims;[23]
- non-practicing Muslims, such as drinkers of wine, one who committed suicide, a fornicator, and so forth;
- children of Muslims and the illegitimate child of a Muslim;
- a miscarried child who has completed four months of development in the womb or has formed the features of a human child; and
- a deceased child in a Muslim nation with unknown parents or in a non-Muslim nation where there are Muslims and there is a possibility that the child belongs to them.

WHAT ABOUT A MISCARRIED CHILD?

The rulings on a miscarried child depend on the child's age and state of development.

---

23. This refers to a Muslim from a different sect or school of thought, such as Hanafi, Maliki, Zaidi, or anyone who is not from the Imami Jafari Twelver school of thought.

- If it has completed four months gestation, it must be washed, camphorated, shrouded, and buried. Funeral prayer is not required.
- If it has not completed four months gestation,
  - and it has not formed the features of a human child, it must be wrapped with a cloth based on obligatory precaution and then buried; or
  - if it has formed the features of a human child, based on obligatory precaution it must be washed, camphorated, shrouded, and buried. Funeral prayer is not required.

CONDITIONS OF WASHING (GHUSL)

What follows are the conditions that must occur when washing the body:

- Removal of impurities from the body of the deceased. It is acceptable to remove the impurities from each body part and wash it (i.e., sequentially) before doing the same for the next body part. Removing impurities from the whole body is not required before commencing the wash.
- The water must be pure and permissible to use (i.e., it must not be stolen or otherwise used without appropriate permission).
- The lote tree leaves (*sidr*) and camphor (*kafur*) must be permissible (*mubah*) to use (i.e., they must not be usurped and permission must have been obtained.)
- Based on recommended precaution, the mortuary washing table, the water draining

conduit, and water container should be permissible (mubah) to use if it does not restrict fulfillment of the rituals.
- From the beginning of the wash until its completion, those washing the body should perform the wash with the sole intention of seeking proximity to God.
- The wash must be performed using the sequential (*tartibi*) method based on obligatory precaution. Therefore, it is not enough to perform an immersive wash (*irtimasi*) on the deceased.

REQUIREMENTS FOR THE PERSON PERFORMING THE WASH

The person performing the wash must meet the following conditions:

- Sanity—they must be sane.
- Islam—they must be a Muslim, and based on obligatory precaution they must also be a Twelver Shia.
- Discerning—the washer may be a child if they are *mumayyiz*[24] or discerning and can perform the wash correctly.
- Same gender—they must be of the same gender; therefore, it is not permissible for a male to wash a female and vice versa, except in the following situations:

---

24. Mumayyiz is the age at which a person possesses understanding of the state of death, gender, and the rules of burial.

- A child—if the deceased is a non-discerning child, and based on recommended precaution the child must not be over the age of three years. Therefore, it is permissible for either gender to wash the child, with or without a garment to cover the private area, and regardless of whether someone of the same gender is available.
- Husband and wife—it is permissible for a husband to wash his wife and vice versa, with a garment to cover the private area or without it, and whether someone of the same gender is available or not. This applies to both permanent and temporary marriages and during the waiting period of a revocable divorce.
- Mahram—anyone whom the person is not permitted to marry due to blood ties, suckling, or marriage, but not from fornication, sodomy, etc. Further, based on obligatory precaution, one should not resort to washing a mahram of the opposite gender unless there is no one from the same gender available. Based on recommended precaution, there should be a garment on the deceased during the washing. It is unlawful to look at the private parts of the deceased or touch them, even if doing so does not invalidate the wash.
- Gender unknown—if it is unknown whether a deceased or part of the body is male or female, either gender may wash it.

After Death

SAME GENDER OR MAHRAM NOT AVAILABLE

What is the ruling if a Twelver Shia of the same gender or a mahram is not available?

There are different possible situations:

- A Twelver Shia Muslim of the same gender or one of the deceased's mahram relatives is not available. In this case a non-Shia Muslim[25] or non-Twelver Shia Muslim of the same gender may perform the wash.
- Neither a Shia Muslim nor a Muslim from other sects is available, but there is a non-Muslim from the People of the Book (e.g., Jewish or Christian) who is of the same gender. In this situation, the non-Muslim from the People of the Book who is of the same gender as the deceased may perform the wash. However, they must perform a ritual wash themselves first and then wash the deceased. Based on recommended precaution, they should make an intention (*niyyah*) to do so if possible, as should the one who requested them to perform the wash. In addition, they should use *kurr* (large amount) water or water that is flowing if possible, or they should not touch the water or the body of the deceased based on a recommended precaution.

---

25. Non-Shia Muslim refers to a different sect or school of thought within the religion of Islam such as Hanafi, Maliki, Zaidi, or someone who is not a Jafari Twelver.

Q: What if a Shia or even a non-Shia Muslim of the same gender becomes available after the non-Muslim completes the wash?
A: If they become available prior to burial, the wash should be repeated based on obligatory precaution.

- Otherwise, the requirement to perform the wash is revoked if a person from the same gender is not available, even from the People of the Book.

How to wash the deceased

The deceased must undergo three washes in the following order:

1. Lote tree leaves (sidr) mixed in water
2. Camphor (kafur) mixed in water
3. Plain water (i.e., not mixed with anything)

- The amount of lote tree leaves (sidr) and camphor (kafur) must not be so much that the water becomes completely mixed (*mudhaf*)[26] (i.e., ceases to be considered plain water). On the other hand, the amount must also not be so minute that the water is considered as not having any sidr or camphor added to it.
- The plain water that is used to perform the third wash must be free from lote tree leaves (sidr) and camphor (kafur). However, there is no problem if a very small amount (i.e.,

---

26. Mixed water (mudhaf) is water that ceases to be plain (*mutlaq*) water, because it is mixed with something else.

debris) remains such that the water is considered unmixed.
- The method of performing these washes is the same as that for janabah, which is to start with the head and neck first, and then the right part of the body along with the private parts followed by the left part of the body with the private parts.
- Fresh or dry lote tree leaves may be used.

Recommended acts of washing

As much as possible, there are several recommended acts that the washer should observe when washing the deceased. These include

- placing the deceased on an elevated place [such as a table];
- placing the deceased in a shaded area;
- turning and facing the deceased towards the direction of the qiblah, the same way they were positioned at the time of death (ihtidar);
- taking off the deceased's long shirt (*qamis*) by sliding it through the legs, and, if the heir permits, even by tearing it if necessary. In addition, the top garment should be placed over the private parts as a cover based on recommended precaution;
- gently extending the deceased's fingers as well as the remainder of their joints;
- washing each part three times during each wash (the head three times, then the right side three times, etc.);

- washing the head with foam that forms upon mixing with the water that is made from lote tree leaves, and the private parts with saltwort (*ashnan*) without touching them directly. Ashnan is a tree from the Chenopodiaceous subfamily that grows in sandy soil; it (or its dried powder) is commonly used for washing clothes and hands. It is in the same family as spinach and chard.[27] It is reported that Imam Jafar al-Sadiq (p) said, "Begin with [washing] the private parts of the deceased, then perform the ablution for prayer on them;"[28]
- wiping the stomach of the deceased with lote tree leaves (sidr) before the first wash, and with camphor (kafur) before the second wash, with the exception that it is detestable (makruh) to do so for a pregnant woman whose unborn child died in her womb;
- the washer standing on the right side of the deceased;
- the presence of a cavity dug for water (runoff); and
- drying the deceased with a clean cloth (prior to shrouding).

---

27. *Al-mujam al-wasit.* (المعجم الوسيط)
28. Al-Hurr al-Amili, *Wasail al-Shia*, vol. 2, p. 491.

DETESTABLE ACTS (MAKRUHAT) WHEN WASHING THE DECEASED

The following are some of the detestable acts that should be avoided while washing the deceased:

- Placing them in a seated position
- Straightening their hair and making them lie between the legs of the washer
- Allowing the water (runoff) to flow into the toilet
- Applying preservatives on their fingernails
- Using hot water, whether it was heated on a fire or by other means, except when no other option is available
- Crossing over the body during the wash

IF LOTE TREE LEAVES OR CAMPHOR ARE NOT AVAILABLE

Q: What is the ruling if lote tree leaves (sidr), camphor (kafur) or both are not available?

A: The following must be observed based on obligatory precaution:

1. The deceased must be washed with plain water as a substitute for the first wash (sidr); this must be performed with the intention of this substitution.
2. The deceased must be washed with plain water as a substitute for the second wash (camphor); this must be performed with the intention of this substitution.
3. The deceased must be washed with plain water as the third wash.

4. Dry ablution (*tayammum*) should also be included thereafter.

Q: What is the ruling if lote tree leaves and camphor become available?
A: If they become available there are two possibilities.

- Prior to burial—the deceased must be washed again.
- After burial—the grave is not to be exhumed solely for the purpose of rewashing the body. However, if the deceased was exhumed for another reason, then based on obligatory precaution they must be rewashed with lote tree leaves, then camphor, and lastly plain water.

Ruling on the drops of water that fall from the dead body

Q: Are the drops of water that fall from the body of the deceased after completion of the first two washes (sidr and kafur) but before the third wash considered pure?
A: The body of the deceased becomes pure only after the completion of the three washes; therefore, any little (*qalil*) water that encounters the body before that point is considered impure (*najis*).

METHOD OF PERFORMING TAYAMMUM

It is acceptable to perform tayammum once on the deceased, and the recommended precaution is to do so three times.

Tayammum must be performed with the hands of the living person, and the recommended precaution is to perform another tayammum using the hands of the deceased if possible.

How to perform tayammum

The washer must strike the earth with their palms, and it is sufficient if they place them on any surface with which tayammum can be performed, such as soil or marble that has some amount of dust on it (i.e., it is not completely wiped free of dust).

Then, all at once, they must wipe the deceased's entire forehead and the temples from the place where the hair of the head grows to the eyebrows, and then the root of the nose. The recommended precaution is to also wipe the eyebrows. Then, wipe the back of the right hand from the wrist to the tip of the fingers with the palm of the left hand, and wipe the back of the left hand from the wrist to the tip of the fingers with the palm of the right hand. The recommended precaution is to strike the earth twice, once for wiping the forehead and the backs of the hands and a second time for the backs of the hands only.

Situations in which tayammum may be performed instead of ghusl

Waiting is required if there is a possibility of performing ghusl. However, if it is certain that washing will not be possible, then it is permissible to perform tayammum. The deceased must be washed if performing it becomes possible prior to the burial. If washing becomes available after having already performed tayammum and completing the burial, it is not permissible to exhume the grave.

If the deceased is taken out of the grave for some other reason, they must be washed based on obligatory precaution.[29] In any case, tayammum is not performed in place of ghusl on the deceased except under the following circumstances:

- There is no water or it is not readily available.
- Washing will lead to flesh falling off the body.

Q: What if the body becomes impure due to either an external impurity or an internal one (e.g., blood) during or after the completion of ghusl, and it is possible to purify it without any hardship while simultaneously preserving the sanctity of the deceased?
A:
- It must be purified if the impurity occurs before placing the body in the grave.
- It must be purified based on obligatory precaution if the impurity occurs after placing the body in the grave.

Q: Is it obligatory to repeat the wash if urine or semen are discharged from the deceased?
A: It is not obligatory to repeat the wash even if this occurs just before placing the deceased in the grave.

---

29. The same rule applies if the deceased was washed with only plain water because sidr and camphor were not available (i.e., in substitution).

After Death

Q: Is it permissible to charge a fee for washing a deceased person?
A: It is not permissible to charge a fee for washing a deceased person based on obligatory precaution. However, a fee may be charged for the water or other things that a person is not obligated by religious law to provide for free.

COMPLETE SEQUENCE OF WASHING

It is recommended for the washer to stand on the right side of the deceased, and thereafter for them to do the following:

1. It is better to cover the private parts of the deceased with a piece of cloth (e.g., a piece of their shirt), and gently extend their fingers and the remainder of their joints.
2. Before performing the actual wash (ghusl)
   - wash the head with the foam taken from the surface of the sidr water (*raghwat al-sidr*) beginning with the right half of the head and then moving to the left;
   - wash the private parts with ashnan without making unlawful contact (i.e., touching the private parts). Place a cover over the private parts;
   - begin by washing half of the deceased's arm three times (the part of the arm that is washed during ablution); and
   - wipe the stomach of the deceased with sidr before the first wash, and wipe it with kafur before the second wash. However, it is

detestable (makruh) to do so for a pregnant woman whose unborn child died in her womb.
3. Wash the head first beginning with the right side, then the left side, and then wash the neck.
4. Wash the right side of the body, washing each part three times for each ghusl (three times with water containing sidr, three times with water containing kafur, etc.).
5. Wash the left side of the body as performed on the right.
6. Dry the deceased's body with a clean towel or cloth after completion of the three washes and before the shrouding.

Ruling on burial of the deceased without performing the obligatory wash

If the deceased was buried without washing, either intentionally or by mistake, it is permissible to exhume the body to wash it. Rather, it is obligatory if it does not entail hardship on those performing the rituals of death, even if they are bothered by just the odor. The same rulings apply if one or two of the washes were left out or were performed incorrectly, whether deliberately or mistakenly. However, the exception of not having to exhume due to hardship does not apply in the case of the person who deliberately buried the deceased without washing them (they must exhume the corpse and wash it even if they are bothered by the odor). However, exhuming the body is not permissible if it entails disrespect or causes damage to the body of the deceased.

2. Application of camphor (tahnit)

It is obligatory to camphorate a deceased Muslim prior to burial. As such, fresh fragrant (i.e., has not lost its scent) powdered camphor or kafur must be applied on the seven parts of the body that rest on the ground during *sujud* (the forehead, palms, knees, and tips of the big toes) by wiping using the whole palm of the hand based on recommended precaution. Moreover, the entire palms of the deceased should be wiped as a precaution and not merely the center. It is better to use seven *mithqal* [approximately 32.48 grams] of camphor in the process, and it is recommended to mix it with a small amount of the soil of Imam Hussain's grave.[30] It is also recommended to wipe the joints, the end of the neck or the part that meets the chest, the soles of the feet, and the backs of the hands [from the wrist to the tip of the fingers]. However, it must not be applied to the parts of the body in a way that is disrespectful to the soil of Imam Hussain's grave.

PERSON(S) RESPONSIBLE FOR CAMPHORATING COSTS

The following are responsible for camphorating costs and are listed in the order of precedence:

1. The deceased would pay if they had prepared and saved for it during their lifetime and mentioned it in their will.
2. The deceased's estate must cover the costs if they were not already acquired, prepared, and set aside by the deceased.

---

30. This refers to soil from land surrounding the holy shrine of Imam Hussain (p).

3. The heirs can pay the costs if the deceased had no estate and if they are able.
4. Muslims in general (i.e., as a community) are responsible for the costs if none of the above are possible.

As for the wife, if she does not direct fulfillment of this requirement with her own wealth in a will, and there is no donor to provide the camphor, then based on obligatory precaution her husband is responsible for the costs of her preparation for burial provided it does not impose hardship on him. This includes the lote tree leaves (sidr) and camphor (kafur).

Camphorating must be done after performing the wash or tayammum (if the circumstances warrant), and either before or during shrouding.

Obligatory Acts Related to Camphorating

Camphorating is to wipe the seven parts of the body that touch the ground during prostration (sujud) with camphor, and the recommended precaution is that this should be done with the palm. The seven places are

1. the forehead;
2. the entire right palm;
3. the entire left palm;
4. the right knee;
5. the left knee;
6. the right big toe; and
7. the left big toe.

The camphor must meet the following conditions:

- It must be permissible to use (not usurped or permission to use was not obtained).
- The powder must be fresh and fragrant.
- It must be pure (*tahir*). The camphor must not be used based on obligatory precaution if it is impure or *mutanajjis*, even if it does not transfer impurity to the body of the deceased.

CASES IN WHICH CAMPHORATING IS NOT MANDATORY

The obligation to camphorate the body of the deceased is revoked in the following two cases:

- Camphor is not available.
- Camphor is not permissible to use (i.e., it is usurped or permission to use was not obtained).

RECOMMENDED ACTS (MUSTAHABBAT) DURING CAMPHORATING

The following acts are recommended when camphorating:

- Camphorating should be done with the palm of the hand based on recommended precaution.
- It is better that the amount of camphor is seven *mithqal sayrafi*[31] [which is about 32.48 grams].
- It is recommended to apply camphor on the joints, manubrium (*lubbah*), chest, soles of the feet, and backs of the hands.

---

31. A mithqal is equal to 4.64 grams.

Detestable acts (makruhat) during camphorating

It is detestable to insert camphor into

- the eyes of the deceased;
- the nose; or
- the ears.

Illustration of camphorating

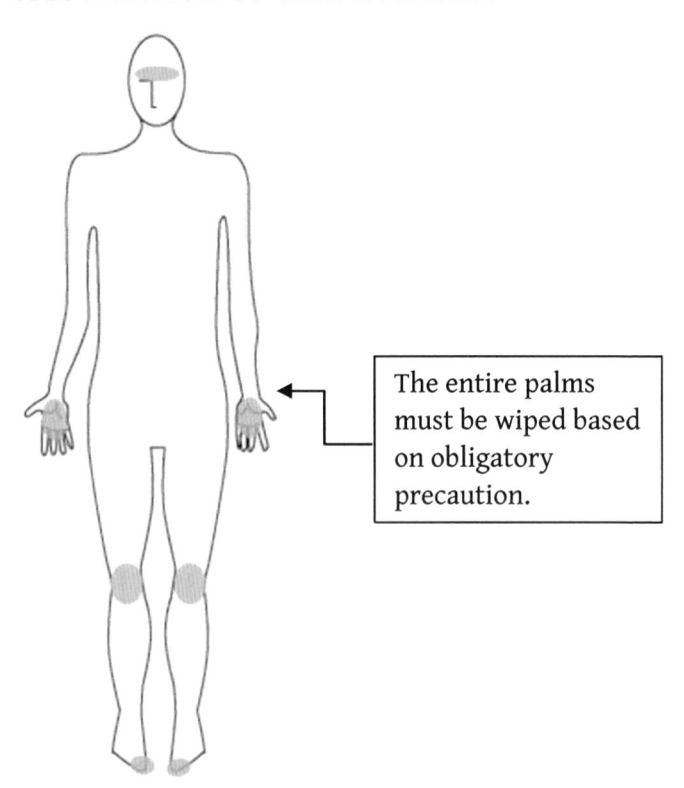

The entire palms must be wiped based on obligatory precaution.

3. Shrouding

METHOD OF SHROUDING

It is obligatory to shroud the deceased in three pieces of cloth after completing the obligatory wash and camphorating them (as mentioned above). These include the following:

1. Loin cloth (*mizar*)
   The length of the loincloth (mizar) must be from the navel to the knees based on obligatory precaution, and it is better if it is from the chest to the feet.
2. Tunic or long shirt (qamis)
   The length of the tunic [long shirt] (qamis) must be from the shoulders to halfway past the shins based on obligatory precaution, and it is better to have it extend to the feet.
3. Full cover (*izar*)
   The full cover (izar) must cover the entire body, and based on obligatory precaution it must be long enough so that it can be tied [and closed] at both ends and wide enough that one side can overlap the other.

THE SHROUDING OF THE WIFE

The husband, irrespective of whether he is young or old; sane or not; or whether he has consummated the marriage with her or not, is responsible for the cost of his wife's shroud, even if she has wealth [to obtain it herself]. This also applies if she is revocably divorced, she did not perform her marital obligations (*nashiz*), or she is a temporary wife.

Conditions of obligating the husband to provide his wife's shroud

The husband is responsible for the cost of his wife's shroud if the following conditions are met:

- The wife dies while her husband is alive; therefore, if they die at the same time, the cost of her shroud does not come out of his estate.
- The shroud is not [already] donated by another person; if this occurs, the husband is not obligated to provide it.
- The wife did not [already] direct in her will that the cost of her shrouding should come from her own wealth. If such a directive exists and is executed, the husband is not obligated to provide her shroud.
- Paying the cost of the shroud does not impose a hardship on the husband. Therefore, if the husband can provide the shroud without hardship, even if it is by borrowing money [to do so] or securing his property (*rahn*), he is obliged to provide it; otherwise it is not obligatory.

PROVIDING THE SHROUD OF A RELATIVE

Providing the shroud of a deceased relative is not obligatory, even if one was responsible for their living expenses when they were alive (e.g., parents). Accordingly, the cost of the shroud comes out of the deceased's estate.

CONDITIONS OF THE SHROUD

The following are conditions that must be fulfilled for the shroud:

- The deceased must be shrouded with something that is considered to be a garment, even if it is made of fur, wool, or the skin of an animal that is lawful to eat.
- It must be permissible to use (not usurped or permission to use was not obtained). This will be explained in the section immediately following this one.
- It must be pure (i.e., it must not be najis or mutanajjis, including the types of *najasah* that are ordinarily permissible on clothes during prayers).
- It must not be made of pure silk. However, it is permissible to use silk that is mixed with other material if the latter is more than the former.
- It must not be woven with gold based on obligatory precaution.
- It must not be made from parts of an animal that is unlawful to eat, nor from the skin of a carcass, even if it is pure.
- The pieces of the shroud must cover and conceal the body of the deceased based on recommended precaution, and it is sufficient if this occurs by putting all the pieces together.

All these conditions except the second (permissibility of use) apply under normal circumstances and may be abandoned or ignored when there is no alternative.

What is meant by permissibility of using the shroud?

Permissibility of using the shroud means

- the garment is not usurped;
- it is not taken without the permission of its owner, unless permission can be obtained by virtue of reasonable appropriate usage or *fahwa*, (for example, if a person uses their brother's shroud for their father); and
- it must not be from money that is due for khums (i.e., if the shroud was purchased and kept for more than one year without using it).

WHAT IF IT IS NOT POSSIBLE TO OBTAIN A COMPLETE SHROUD?

It is sufficient to use what is available if obtaining the three pieces of the shroud is not possible.

1. Preference must be given to the full cover (izar) if only one of the three pieces can be obtained.
2. If it is only possible to obtain either the loincloth (mizar) or the long shirt (qamis), preference must be given to the latter.
3. If only one piece is available and it is only large enough to conceal the genitals, then it must be used to do so.
4. If the amount of shroud is only large enough to conceal either the genitals or the buttocks, it must be used to conceal the former.

What are the private parts (those parts that must be concealed)?

The private parts that must be concealed are as follows:

- Male—penis, testicles, and anus
- Female—the entire body including the hair. This excludes
  - the face—the part that is not covered by the veil that extends to the chest; every part that is not typically washed during ablution should be covered based on recommended precaution;
  - the hands—the wrist to the tips of the fingers; and
  - the feet—the soles and the upper parts.

It is best to conceal a little bit more than the limits defined above.

PERMISSIBILITY TO SHROUD THE DECEASED WHEN ACCEPTABLE SHROUDS ARE UNAVAILABLE

Although it is not permissible to shroud the deceased in pure silk, a shroud that is impure, a shroud woven with gold (based on obligatory precaution), one made from the parts of an animal that is unlawful to eat, or one that is usurped, even if it is the only thing available, these shrouds may be used when no other acceptable option is available. Under these circumstances, it is permissible to use any of the aforementioned shrouds, and if more than one is available, preference must be given based on the following order:

1. If only one is available, it must be used.
2. If there are two shrouds available, one made of an inherent impurity (najis) (e.g., skin of a dog) and another that is ordinarily permissible (e.g., cotton garment) but has come into contact with an intrinsic impurity and has hence become mutanajjis, the latter must be used.
3. If there are two shrouds, either one made of an intrinsic impurity (najis) or one that is ordinarily permissible but has come into contact with an intrinsic impurity and become mutanajjis, and a shroud made of pure silk, the one made of pure silk must be used.
4. If there is an alternative (e.g., woven with gold or taken from animal not lawful to eat) it must be used in place of the three (najis, mutanajjis, pure silk).
5. If there are two shrouds, one made from an animal that is unlawful to eat and the other woven with gold, either of the two may be used, and the recommended precaution is to use both.

It is permissible to shroud the deceased with a garment that is silk mixed with other material if the amount of the latter is greater in the shroud's composition.

Purifying the Shroud

If the shroud becomes impure, whether from the body of the deceased or something else, the impurity must be removed, even after laying the body in the grave. This should be done by either washing the shroud or cutting and removing the part that has become impure if it does not shorten it and expose the body. If washing away the impurity from the shroud or cutting it out is not possible, even after laying the body in the grave, it must be replaced if doing so is possible.

Recommended acts related to shrouding (mustahabbat)

Men

It is recommended to wrap the head of the deceased with a turban that has two tails and lay the tails on the chest under the chin by placing the right tail on the left of the body and the left on the right.

Women

The following are recommended for women:

- A head cover that is sufficiently sized to cover the head and neck
- A strip of cloth that is tied across the chest to the back
- The deceased's vagina should be stuffed if there is fear of discharge.

Men and women

The following actions are recommended for both men and women:

- Tie a strip of cloth around the mid-body of the deceased.
- Wrap a strip of cloth around the thighs.
- A large piece of garment should be wrapped over the entire body (over the full cover

izar]). It is best if the outer garment is made of Yemenite burda.
- Place a cotton pad, or similar material if cotton is not available, between the buttocks to conceal the private parts, and apply some camphor to it.
- Stuff the anus and nostrils.
- Place two fresh branches in the shroud with the deceased (more on this later in the section entitled "Recommended Two Twigs").

General recommendations (mustahabbat) for the shroud

Recommendations for the shroud are as follows:

- Good quality
- Made of cotton
- White
- Purchased with pure (lawful) money
- A garment that the deceased used in the state of *ihram* or prayed in
- Apply camphor and *acorus*[32] to it.
- Use threads from the shroud itself if it needs to be stitched.
- Write on the edge of the shroud, "name of the deceased, son/daughter of name of their father, bears witness that there is no God but Allah the One without a partner and Muhammad is the messenger of God." In addition, write the names of the twelve holy

---

32. A type of grassy-leaved plant commonly known as sweet flag.

Imams one after another and declare in writing that they are the close servants of Allah (*awlia*) and successors of His messenger and that resurrection, reward, and retribution are undeniable truths.

- Write Duas al-Jawshan, al-Saghir, and al-Kabir on the shroud. Additionally, it is permissible to bury the deceased with a shroud that has the Holy Quran written on it, with the condition that it is done in a way that ensures the part of the shroud with the verses is safe from becoming impure from blood or other impurities. For example, this may be done by writing the verses on the edge of the full cover (izar) on the side of the deceased's head or writing it on a separate sheet of cloth and placing it on the deceased's chest.
- Cross the right side of the outermost garment cover over the left side and the left side over the right.
- The person shrouding the deceased should be in a state of purity (e.g., be in the state of wudu).
- If the person who washed the deceased is also the one shrouding them, they should wash their arms three times from the shoulders down, their legs up to the knees, and every part of their body that has become impure.
- Face the deceased towards the qiblah during the shrouding procedure, and it is better to lay them in the position they would be in during the funeral prayer (salat al-mayyit).

- It is recommended for every living person to prepare a shroud for themselves prior to their death and gaze at it regularly.

DETESTABLE ACTS RELATED TO SHROUDING

There are specific acts with respect to shrouding the deceased that should be avoided, which include

- cutting the shroud with iron;[33]
- adding a sleeve or buttons to the shroud;
- perfuming the shroud with anything other than camphor or acorus;
- using black or any color other than white;
- using a shroud made of linen or mixed with silk;
- bargaining when buying the shroud;
- wrapping the turban without including a tail (i.e., draped over the chest);
- using a dirty shroud; or
- using a stitched or sewn shroud.

---

33. This includes cutting it with scissors or a knife.

After Death

ILLUSTRATION OF THE OBLIGATORY PIECES OF THE SHROUD

1. **First piece:** Loin cloth (mizar)
2. **Second Piece:** Tunic [long shirt] (qamis)
3. **Third Piece:** Full cover (izar)

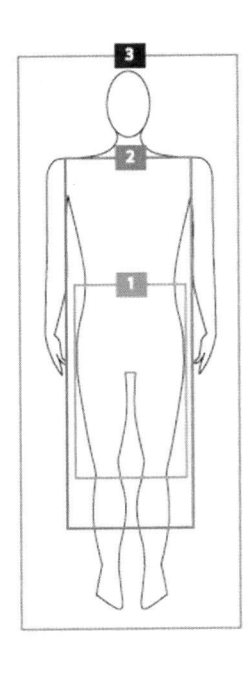

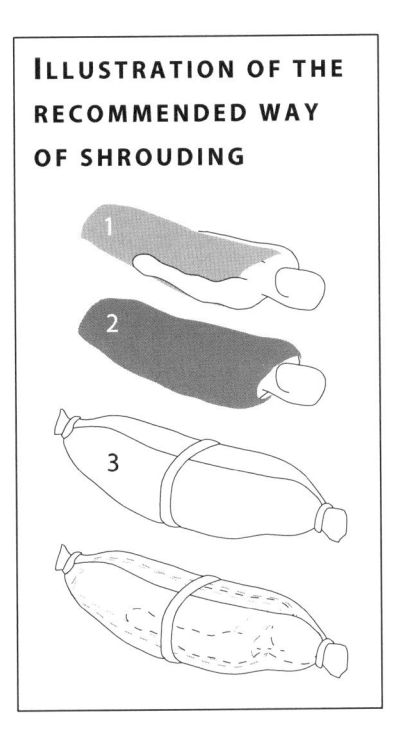

ILLUSTRATION OF THE RECOMMENDED WAY OF SHROUDING

4. Funeral Prayer (salat al-mayyit)

Funeral prayer (salat al-mayyit) is obligatory for the guardian of the deceased or their executor, either by performing it themselves or hiring someone to do so. Permission of the guardian or executor is not needed if they abstain or do not give permission for others to carry out the prayer. In such a case it becomes obligatory for all others (wajib kifai) if no one else fulfills the requirement.

After completing the washing, camphorating, and shrouding, funeral prayer must be performed on every deceased Muslim before the burial as follows:

- Male or female
- Shia Twelver or non-Shia Twelver, just or unjust
- One who committed suicide, irrespective of whether they were sane or insane
- A child if they understood prayer. If one doubts whether the child knew prayer or not, the criterion is completion of six lunar years. Otherwise, it is not obligatory to perform funeral prayer for a child.

It is not permissible to perform funeral prayer for a child who does not understand prayer based on obligatory precaution. However, the funeral prayer may be performed with *niyyah al-raja* (with the intention of hoping that it is ordained by God).

CONDITIONS FOR THE FUNERAL PRAYER

The following conditions must be met for the funeral prayer to be valid:

- Guardian's consent. However, their consent is not required if they refrain from performing the funeral prayer or appointing another person to do so. Similarly, consent is not required if the deceased made a will stipulating a specific individual to perform the funeral prayer.
- Intention of worship (niyyah). Performing the funeral prayer must be done with an intention of and for the sake of attaining nearness to Almighty God because the funeral prayer is an act of worship. As such, the deceased must be specified in a way that eliminates any obscurity at the time of making the intention.
- Presence of the deceased's body. The funeral prayer cannot be performed if the body of the deceased is not present.
- The person performing the funeral prayer must face the direction of the qiblah if they can do so.
- The person performing the funeral prayer must stand; the prayer is not proper except when done in the standing position, unless that is not physically possible.
- The head of the deceased must be on the right side of the person performing the prayer and the feet to the left.
- The deceased must be laid on their back.

- The person performing the prayer must stand behind the deceased with others lined up on either side of them. If they are performing the funeral prayer on more than one deceased lined up next to each other, they can do so adjacent to one in the middle of the line, taking into account the number of individuals being prayed for when reciting the supplications.
- There must not be any barrier such as a veil or a wall (such that they would not be considered in a state of standing to pray for the deceased) between the person performing the prayer and the deceased. However, there is no problem in having a casket or another deceased in between.
- There must be a close succession (continuity) between the *takbirat* and invocations such that there is no long pause or interruption that would annul the form of prayer.
- The funeral prayer must be performed before the burial and after the completion of washing, camphorating, and shrouding, when they are obligatory to perform or in circumstances when only some are required.
- The deceased's private parts must be covered, by any appropriate means (i.e., if there is no shroud available).
- Speaking, laughing, and turning towards the back or away from the direction of the qiblah during the funeral prayer should be avoided based on obligatory precaution.

After Death

Rulings for a congregational funeral prayer

There are several matters that should be observed in a congregational funeral prayer.

- Funeral prayer is recommended in congregation.
- The imam (leader of the prayer) should meet the same criteria that are required for congregational prayer based on obligatory precaution. These include religious maturity (bulugh), sanity, being a Shia, being of legitimate birth, and they must be capable of reciting the required supplications in proper Arabic with correct recitation. In addition, the imam must be a male if those following him in prayer are males. Also, based on recommended precaution the imam should be just [although this condition is not required].
- The imam's recitation does not suffice for the followers' in the required acts of prayer, therefore everyone must recite the takbirat and supplications on their own.
- The imam must stand behind the deceased, and it is recommended for them to do so adjacent to the middle of the body if the deceased is a male and adjacent to the chest if the deceased is a female. If there are two deceased individuals, a male and a female, the male should be closer to the imam and the female should be placed in a way that her chest is adjacent to the middle part of the male as a recommended precaution. It is also

permissible to place them in one line where the head of one is adjacent to the rear of the other casket and have the imam stand in the middle.
- It is better for the imam to say *"al-salat, al-salat, al-salat"* before starting the prayer.
- It is recommended for the imam to recite the takbirat and supplications in a loud voice and for the followers to recite in a low voice.
- It is recommended for the follower(s) to stand behind the imam and not to their side, even if there is only one person.
- For the validity of the congregational funeral prayer, the followers must observe the conditions that preserve the form of a general congregational prayer such as not being far from the imam without a connection. The other conditions of congregational prayer are not required in the congregational funeral prayer.
- There is no problem if the distance between the imam and a follower is large if there is a connection to the congregation in a long, albeit crooked, row or though connection with subsequent rows.
- It is permissible for a woman to lead a women's congregational funeral prayer, and she must stand in the middle of the line and not in front of the congregation based on obligatory precaution.

After Death

WHAT IS NOT REQUIRED IN FUNERAL PRAYER

Based on recommended precaution, the conditions of prayer[34] should be observed; however, the following conditions are not required for the validity of the funeral prayer:

- Being in the state of purity (performing ablution [wudu], ritual bath [ghusl], or dry ablution [tayammum]). Similarly, purity of the body and clothing is not a requirement.
- Permissibility of use (*ibaha*) of the clothing for the people performing the prayer and place where the funeral prayer is performed.

THE ETIQUETTE OF FUNERAL PRAYER AND RECOMMENDED ACTS RELATED TO IT

- It is recommended for the person performing the funeral prayer to be in a state of purity (e.g., in the state of wudu). It is also permissible to perform tayammum, even if water is available. This is the case when time does not permit them to perform wudu or ghusl based on obligatory precaution.
- It is recommended for the imam or the individual who is performing the funeral prayer to stand alone adjacent to the middle of the body if the deceased is a male and adjacent to the chest if the deceased is a female.
- It is recommended to raise the hands when saying *Allahu akbar* in all the takbirat.

---

34. This includes conditions like being in the state of purity.

- It is recommended for the imam to recite the takbirat and supplications in a loud voice and for the follower(s) to recite in a low voice.
- It is recommended to select a place where people usually gather to assemble as many people as possible to perform the funeral prayer.
- It is recommended that the follower(s) stand behind the imam and not to the side, even if they are only one person.
- It is recommended to be diligent in praying for the deceased and believers.
- It is recommended to perform the funeral prayer in a congregational form.
- If a discerning child (mumayyiz) prays for a deceased person, their prayer can take the place of a baligh person; however, the recommended precaution is that a baligh person should perform the prayer.
- It is recommended for the person performing the funeral prayer to stand barefoot.

METHOD OF PERFORMING FUNERAL PRAYER

The funeral prayer involves five takbirat and supplications for the deceased. Although the supplications must follow one of the first four takbirat (the fifth takbirah ends the prayer) with the other three takbirat followed by *salawat* on the Prophet (pbuh&hp), *shahadatayn*, and supplication for all the believers and praise for God, it is a recommended precaution to use the following method:

After Death

First: Niyyah (intention) – The person praying should make an intention of attaining nearness (*qurbah*) to God, should specify the deceased in a way that eliminates any obscurity (i.e., about their identity), and should use the correct pronoun with respect to their gender. For example, the person performing the prayer makes the intention, "I am performing the funeral prayer (salat al-mayyit) on [name of the deceased] to attain nearness to God Almighty." Moreover, verbal articulation is not required; presence of the intention in the heart is enough as in all other acts of worship. If the person praying does not know the gender of the deceased, they may use the pronoun according to what they observe from the coffin and body in terms of the possible gender. It is also permissible to do so even if one knows.

Second: Reciting *takbir* five times in the following method:

1. Allahu akbar (الله أكبر), then testify by saying "I bear witness that there is no God but Allah the One for whom there is no partner, and I bear witness that Muhammad is His servant and messenger. He [God] sent him with the truth as a bearer of good news and as a warner before the advent of the hour [Day of Resurrection]."

   أَشهدُ أَنْ لا إِلهَ إِلاّ الله، وَحْدَهُ لا شَريكَ لَهُ، وأشهدُ أَنَّ محمّداً عبدُهُ وَرَسُولُه، أرسَلَهُ بِالحَقِّ بَشيراً وَنَذيراً بَينَ يَدَيْ السَّاعَة.

2. Allahu akbar, (then recite) "Oh God, exalt Mohammad and the progeny of Muhammad,

bestow your blessings upon Muhammad and the progeny of Muhammad, and have mercy on Muhammad and the progeny of Muhammad, the best of exaltation, blessings, and mercy that you bestowed upon Abraham and the progeny of Abraham. You are certainly praiseworthy and glorified, and exalt [oh God] all of the prophets, messengers, witnesses, the truthful, and all of the righteous servants of God."

اللّهُمَّ صَلِّ على محمّدٍ وَآلِ محمدٍ وَبارِكْ على محمدٍ وَآلِ محمدٍ، وَارْحَمْ محمداً وَآلَ محمّدٍ، كَأفْضَلِ ما صَلَّيْتَ وَبارَكْتَ وَتَرَحَّمْتَ على إبراهيمَ وَآلِ إبراهيمَ، إنَّكَ حَميدٌ مَجيدٌ، وَصَلِّ عَلى جَميعَ الأنبياءِ والمرسَلينَ والشُّهداءِ والصِّدِّيقينَ وَجَميعِ عِبادِ اللهِ الصَّالحينَ.

3. Allahu akbar, (then recite) "Oh God, forgive the believing men and believing women, the Muslim men and the Muslim women, the living from among them and the dead. And continue [oh God] the connection of good between them and us. Indeed, You answer the supplications and You have power over everything."

اللّهُمَّ اغْفِرْ لِلْمُؤْمِنِيْنَ وَالْمُؤْمِنَاتِ، وَالْمُسْلِمِينَ وَالْمُسْلِمَاتِ، الأحْيَاءِ مِنْهُمْ وَالأمْوَاتِ، تَابِعِ اللّهُمَّ بَيْنَنَا وَبَيْنَهُمْ بِالْخَيْرَاتِ، إنَّكَ مُجِيْبُ الدَّعَوَاتِ إنَّكَ عَلَى كُلِّ شَيءٍ قَدِيرٍ.

After Death

4. Allahu Akbar, (then recite for the deceased) "Oh God, indeed this deceased laying in front of us is Your servant, son/daughter of Your servant and son/daughter of Your maidservant. He/she has become Your guest, and You are the best of hosts. Oh God, we do not know anything except good from him/her and You are more knowing of him/her than us. Oh God, if he/she had been a doer of good, increase his/her good deeds, and if he/she had been a sinner, overlook him/her [by not punishing him/her] and forgive his/her sins. Oh, God place him/her with the highest of the high in rank, and be his/her replacement for his/her household, Oh Most Merciful."

اللَّهُمَّ إِنَّ هَذَا [هذِهِ] الْمُسَجَّى الْمُسَجَّاةُ] قُدَّامَنَا عَبْدُكَ [أَمَتُكَ] وَابْنُ [وَابْنَةُ] عَبْدِكَ وَابْنُ [وَابْنَةُ] أَمَتِكَ، نَزَلَ [نَزَلَتْ] بِكَ وَأَنْتَ خَيْرُ مَنْزُولٍ بِهِ. اللَّهُمَّ إِنَّا لَا نَعْلَمُ مِنْهُ [مِنْهَا] إِلَّا خَيْراً وَأَنْتَ أَعْلَمُ بِهِ [بِهَا] مِنَّا، اللَّهُمَّ إِنْ كَانَ [كَانَتْ] مُحْسِناً [مُحْسِنَةً] فَزِدْ فِي إِحْسَانِهِ [إِحْسَانِهَا]، وَإِنْ كَانَ مُسِيئاً [مُسِيئَةً] فَتَجَاوَزْ عَنْ سَيِّئَاتِهِ [سَيِّئَاتِهَا] وَاغْفِرْ لَهُ [لَهَا]. اللَّهُمَّ اجْعَلْهُ [اجْعَلْهَا] عِنْدَكَ فِي أَعْلَى عِلِّيِّينَ وَاخْلُفْ عَلَى أَهْلِهِ [أَهْلِهَا] فِي الْغَابِرِينَ وَارْحَمْهُ [وَارْحَمْهَا] بِرَحْمَتِكَ يَا أَرْحَمَ الرَّاحِمِينَ.

If the deceased is a child, the following supplication should be recited, "Oh God, make him/her for his/her parents and for us a boon, bountiful [goodness], and reward."

5. Allahu akbar (with this fifth takbir the funeral prayer is complete).

Rulings related to repeating the funeral prayer

The following are rulings for when to repeat the funeral prayer:

- If a person doubts whether they performed the funeral prayer, they must perform it.
- If a person performed the funeral prayer but doubts whether they performed it correctly, they should consider it correct and repeating it is not required.
- If a person determines that the funeral prayer they performed was invalid, they must repeat it.

Q: What is the ruling on a non-Shia Muslim's funeral prayer for one of the relatives [of a Shia] who is also a non-Shia?
A: If the guardian of the deceased was a Shia Muslim, they must perform the funeral prayer, otherwise it is not obligatory to repeat it.

Ruling on burying the deceased without performing a valid funeral prayer

It is not permissible to exhume the body to pray over the deceased if they were buried without a valid funeral prayer. Moreover, it is [religiously] problematic to pray over them while the body is in the grave. Therefore, one should perform it with the intention of *raja* (hoping that God ordained it) based on obligatory precaution.

Ruling on repeating the funeral prayer over the deceased

It is permissible to repeat the funeral prayer over the same deceased, although some jurists have said that it is makruh (detestable) unless the deceased was a person of knowledge, piety, and religious honor.

RULINGS RELATED TO A WOMAN PERFORMING FUNERAL PRAYER

- If the guardian of the deceased is a woman, she can perform the funeral prayer, and it is permissible for her to give permission to another person, male or female, to perform the prayer.
- If the guardian of the deceased was not a woman, it is permissible for a woman to lead a congregation of women in funeral prayer if one of them does not have precedence over the rest. Based on obligatory precaution, the woman leading the prayer should stand in the middle of the first line and not in front of them.

PARTICIPATING IN FUNERAL PROCESSIONS

The virtue of attending funeral processions has been related in many narrations. For example, it is narrated that Imam Muhammad al-Baqir (p) said, "One who follows a funeral procession will be given four intercessions on the day of resurrection, and whatever he says [in supplication for the deceased], the angel will say 'the same will be for you.'"[35] In another narration, it is related that Imam al-Sadiq (p) said, "the first gift that a believer is able to bestow [others after his death] is that those who follow his funeral procession are forgiven."[36]

Recommended acts related to participating in a funeral procession

The following acts are recommended for funeral processions :

- It is recommended for the guardian of the deceased believer to notify other believers about the death so they can attend the funeral procession.
- It is recommended for the believers to attend the funeral procession of a believer.
- The grieving mourner should walk barefoot and not wear a cloak.

Etiquette of attending a funeral procession

There are many etiquette practices for funeral processions that include the following:

- When looking at the coffin, it is recommended to say, "We belong to God and to Him we shall

---

35. Shaykh al-Kulayni, *Al-kafi*, vol. 3, p. 173.
36. Shaykh al-Kulayni, *Al-kafi*, vol. 3, p. 173.

return; this is what God and His messenger have promised us, and indeed it is true what God and His messenger have said. Oh God, increase our faith and submission. All praise is to God whose might ordained and subdued His servants with death." This recommendation is not limited to the participants in the funeral procession, but also anyone who observes it.

- Walk behind the deceased or at their side.
- Be humble and contemplate [about the hereafter and one's responsibility before God].
- Carry the body of the deceased on the shoulder. It is recommended that each person carries the stretcher from its four sides, and it is better to start with the front (the direction it is being carried) right of the corpse and place it on the right shoulder, then the back right of the corpse on the right shoulder, followed by the back left on the left shoulder, and finally the left front on the left shoulder.
- The individuals carrying the deceased should say, "In the name of God and may peace and blessings be upon Muhammad and the progeny of Muhammad. Oh God, forgive the believing men and believing women."
- The deceased should be placed near the grave at a distance of two to three yards or more then transferred gradually in three stages so

that the deceased can be prepared for the grave.[37]
- If the deceased is a male, the body should be placed such that the head is at the foot of the grave; it is then lowered headfirst into the grave.
- If the deceased is a female, the body should be placed lengthwise next to the grave and thereafter facing the qiblah.

Detestable acts (makruhat) during a funeral procession

The following are detestable acts to avoid during a funeral procession:

- Laughing, playing, and engaging in acts of amusement
- Walking at a fast pace that would be considered leaving the deceased behind
- Walking in front of the deceased (i.e., at the head of the casket)
- Riding a vehicle or other means of transportation while participating in the procession
- Talking, other than remembrance of God, supplication, and seeking forgiveness
- Removal of the cloak (i.e., as a sign of mourning) by anyone other than the bereaved

---

37. Although the body is no longer alive, this procedure is likely performed because the deceased is transiting to the next world that is unfamiliar and bewildering from a metaphysical perspective.

After Death

- Placing the deceased into the grave all at once
- Women participating in funeral processions, even if the deceased is a woman
- Showing any sign of despair (e.g., striking the thigh with the hand or striking one hand on the other)

5. Burial

RULINGS RELATED TO THE BURIAL

The following are rulings related to who must be buried:

- It is obligatory to bury a deceased Muslim.
- It is obligatory to bury the miscarried child of a Muslim who has completed four months after washing, camphorating, and shrouding the child's body. However, funeral prayers are not performed.
- If the miscarried child is less than four months but has developed the physical form of a human child, the body must be washed, camphorated, and shrouded based on obligatory precaution.
- If the miscarried child is less than four months and does not have the physical form of a human child, the child should be wrapped in a piece of cloth and buried based on obligatory precaution (i.e., no washing, camphorating, and shrouding is required).

Method of burial

The deceased must be buried in a pit in the ground (i.e., the grave). It is not permissible to place and [permanently] leave them above the ground, as in an above-ground mausoleum or crypt, nor is it allowed to leave them in a coffin without burial. It is sufficient to bury the deceased in a pit under the ground that preserves the body from [being desecrated by] wild animals and causing distress to people due to the odor of the corpse.

- It is a recommended precaution that the grave should, based on its depth, fulfill the aforementioned conditions.
- The deceased must be placed in the grave on their right side with their face towards the direction of the qiblah.

Temporary holding prior to burial

Based on obligatory precaution, it is not permissible to inter or hold up the burial of the deceased by placing them on the ground and building a mausoleum over them as a prelude to transferring the body to the holy sites for burial. Similarly, it is not permissible, based on obligatory precaution, to keep the deceased in a morgue freezer or a similar container for a long period without a dire necessity.

Transferring the body of the deceased

- It is detestable (makruh) to transfer the deceased from the area or town where they died to another place, except for the holy sites

After Death

and honorable places. In fact, it is recommended to do so in the holy cities of Najaf and Karbala, and the other holy sites of the infallibles (p).[38] It is reported in some narrations that burial in the valley of peace (Wadi al-Salam) in the holy city of Najaf prevents the torment of the grave and the accounting of Munkar and Nakir, the two angels who take an account of the person in the grave.

- It is not permissible to transfer the body of the deceased to the holy cities of Najaf, Karbala, or other sites, based on obligatory precaution, if it entails delaying the burial in such a way that the body decomposes.
- The rule establishing detestability of transferring the deceased, and thus permissibility of doing so, is based on the act of transferring not being contingent on exhumation, or if the body somehow appears [above ground] without exhumation. The ruling related to transferring contingent on exhuming the deceased will be explained later in this booklet.

Q: Certain entities that provide a service of transferring bodies from Western countries to countries like Iraq and Lebanon sometimes withdraw the blood of the deceased before placing the body in the morgue freezer and then send it by plane to the desired country. Sometimes they excise the deceased's

---

38. The delay due to a potential transfer of the deceased should not be so long as to result in decay and decomposition of the body.

stomach, remove the intestines, and apply chemical preservatives so that the body does not decay prior to placing it in the freezer. At other times, a chemical substance is spread through the body via the blood vessels to stop decay and decomposition. Are these procedures permissible? If this is not permissible, does this mean that the will of the deceased to be transferred to their homeland or to Najaf for burial becomes void?

A: Withdrawing the blood and entrails of the deceased is not permissible; however, injecting a chemical substance into the blood vessels is permissible. If transferring the body is directed in the will, but it requires withdrawing the blood or entrails, the will cannot be executed.

PLACE OF BURIAL

The following conditions must be observed for the place of burial:

- The place of burial must be permissible to use (mubah); therefore, it is not permissible to bury the deceased in a place without the permission of its owner.
- It is not permissible to bury in a place that has been endowed (waqf) for purposes other than burial such as schools, mosques, and hussainiyyat (Islamic Centers), even if the guardian of those charitable endowments authorizes it. This is the case if burial damages or infringes on the sanctity of the endowment or conflicts with the purpose for which it was endowed. Otherwise, the rule of

impermissibility is based on obligatory precaution.
- It is not permissible to bury a Muslim in the cemeteries of non-Muslims and vice versa.
- It is not permissible to bury a Muslim in a place that infringes on their sanctity such as in an area of waste or sewers.
- If a pregnant non-Muslim woman dies along with the unborn fetus or child from a Muslim father, the woman must be placed in the grave on her left side with her back facing the qiblah (i.e., with the intent that the front of the baby faces qiblah). The same applies, based on recommended precaution, if the soul (ruh) has not yet entered the fetus.
- It is not permissible to dig an occupied grave to bury another corpse, unless the grave is very old and the first corpse has completely decomposed. If the grave is already open, then it is permissible to use it for burial of an additional corpse, if this does not entail an unlawful act such as using the property of others without justification.

About the sepulchre (*lahd*)

In this section, the burial ground, the person responsible for burial rites, and the recommended acts after burial will be covered.

Digging the sepulchre[39] is dependent on the type of earth involved, as follows:

- Hard ground
  A sepulchre should be dug to a depth equal to the height of an average person in a seated position.
- Soft ground
  1. A pit should be dug in the center of the grave (i.e., a pit inside of a pit).
  2. The deceased should be placed in the pit.
  3. Then, place a wooden plank of wood over the deceased, and place the soil over it.

RECOMMENDATIONS FOR THE PERSON RESPONSIBLE FOR BURIAL RITES

The following are recommended for the person responsible for burial rites:

- The person responsible for burial rites should be the guardian of the deceased (wali) or the person who is religiously in the same category as the guardian for this purpose.
- If the deceased is a woman, the person responsible for burial rites should be a mahram to her, and the grave should be covered with a garment when the body is interred.
- While placing the deceased in the sepulchre (lahd), the person responsible for burial rites

---

39. The sepulchre is a narrow trench within the grave where the body is positioned.

(a male) should be barefoot, with their shirt open, and not wearing anything on their head.

DEPTH OF THE GRAVE

It is recommended that the depth of the grave is equal to the height of an average person or to the shoulder.

THE COFFIN

Q: In non-Muslim countries the deceased is often placed in a coffin that is then placed inside the grave. Is there a problem in this?
A: There is no problem in placing the deceased in a coffin and then burying it. However, the conditions of burial, such as positioning the deceased on their right side facing the direction of the qiblah, must be observed.

RECOMMENDATIONS FOR THE CONDITION OF THE CORPSE

What follows are recommendations for the placement of the corpse and actions taken during the burial:

1. The shroud tie from the side of the head should be opened after the body is placed in the grave.
2. The face should be uncovered.
3. The back of the corpse should be supported with a brick or within a sepulchre (lahd) so that it does not lie on its back.
4. A pillow made of soil should be placed under the right side of the head of the corpse. If this is not possible due to the corpse being inside a

coffin, the pillow should be placed under the head inside the coffin.
5. The right cheek of the corpse should lay on the earth. If this is not possible due to the corpse being inside a coffin, soil should be placed under the cheek inside the coffin.
6. Place some of the soil from the grave of Imam Hussain (p) with the body.
7. Inculcate the testimonies of faith and the acknowledgement of the twelve Imams (pbut) (talqin).
8. The sepulchre should be closed with bricks.
9. The person responsible for burial rites should exit the grave from the side of the corpse's feet.
10. The non-relatives of the deceased should throw earth [into the grave] with the back of their hands.
11. After filling the grave with earth, it should be raised above the surrounding ground by a length of three fingers, either closed or spread.
12. Make the grave four-sided (i.e., with four corners).
13. Splash water on the grave in a circular motion, beginning from the side of the head. If some water remains, it should be splashed on the center of the grave.
14. After splashing water, those who are present should place their hands on the grave and press into the soil with their fingers. The fingers should be pressed deeper into the grave if the deceased is a Hashimite (from the children of Hashim the grandfather of the

prophet [pbuh&hp]). This recommendation applies more for those who did not attend the funeral prayer.
15. Supplicate to God and ask His mercy for the deceased. For example, "Oh God, make the ground spacious for him/her on both of his/her sides, and raise his/her spirit (ruh) to be among the spirits of the believers in the high ranks and join him/her with the righteous." Also ask God to forgive the deceased and recite Surat al-Qadr seven times for them.
16. The guardian should inculcate (talqin) the deceased or authorize someone to do it aloud after everyone leaves.
17. A rock or a sign should be placed on the grave with the name of the deceased written on it.

Recommended Two Twigs

Among the recommended acts in the school of Ahl al-Bayt (pbut) is to place two twigs with the deceased, whether they are young or old, male or female, good or evil [in their actions], or one whom you fear will be tormented in the grave or not. It was reported, "the twig (*jaridah*) benefits the believer and the non-believer, the good-doer and the evil-doer; as long as it is wet, the torment of the grave is removed from the deceased."[40] In another narration, it was reported that the Prophet (pbuh&hp) had passed by a grave in which the deceased was being punished. The Prophet (pbuh&hp) brought a twig and cut it into two pieces,

---

40. Al-Sayyid al-Burujurdi, *Jami ahadith al-Shia*, vol. 3, p. 259.

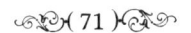

then placed one over the side of the head and one over the foot, and he said that the torment of this deceased shall be reduced as long as they [the twigs] are wet.[41]

- It is recommended to place two freshly cut twigs with the deceased in the grave, and it is better to place them in the following manner:
    - The first twig should be placed on the right side, with one end at the collarbone and up against the deceased's body.
    - The second twig should be placed on the left side, with one end at the collarbone over the long shirt (qamis) and under the full cover (izar).
    - If there is only one twig available, it should be placed on the right side of the deceased.
- It is recommended that the twigs be from palm trees. If those are not available, then lote tree (sidr), and if not those, then pomegranate tree. If none of these are available, then any fresh twig will suffice.
- If the two twigs were not placed in the grave due to forgetfulness or some other reason, it is better to place them over the grave, one near the head and the other near the feet.
- It is best to write the same writing that is written on the edges of the shroud (as explained earlier) on the two twigs, and it is then necessary to prevent the writing from coming into contact with impurities such as

---

41. Al-Sayyid al-Yazdi, *Al-urwat al-wuthqa*, vol. 2, p. 83.

blood by wrapping it with plastic or other such material.
- It is also best to write the deceased's name and their father's name; that they testify that "There is no God but Allah, and Muhammad is His messenger (pbuh&hp), and the Imams (pbut) after him are his successors;" and write the names of the Imams (pbut).
- It is best if the length of the twig is an arm's length, and less than that is also enough.

WHEN THE DIRECTION OF THE QIBLAH IS UNCERTAIN

When the direction of the qiblah is uncertain and the burial cannot be delayed until its location or some estimation thereof is determined, the most probable direction must be acted upon after a reasonable investigation. If that too is not possible, then the requirement of facing the qiblah is revoked.

GENERAL DETESTABLE ACTS (MAKRUHAT)

The following are other detestable acts:

- Burying two corpses in one grave
- A father going inside the grave of his son
- A non-mahram entering into the grave of a woman
- Placing the corpse into the grave suddenly without placing it near the grave and after having it lifted and put down on the ground in stages
- A relative throwing soil on the deceased

- Mounting teak in the grave without a need for it
- Plastering the grave, coating it with mud, or making it into a pyramid shape
- Walking, sitting, or leaning on the grave
- Building on top of it or rebuilding it after it has become very old, except for the graves of prophets, successors, scholars, and righteous individuals
- Laughing in cemeteries

RULING ON EXHUMING THE GRAVE

It is unlawful to exhume the grave of a Muslim in a way that their body becomes visible, unless it is certain that the corpse has [decomposed and] transformed into earth, whether the deceased was young or old, sane or insane, with the following exceptions:

- If they were buried in a place that entails disrespect to them, such as a waste site or a sewer, or in a place that poses harm to their body, such as being attacked by a wild animal or an enemy
- There is a reason that requires seeing the deceased that is as or more important, such as saving the life of a Muslim.
- If usurped property, such as a ring or something similar, was buried with them. In this case, the grave may be exhumed to bring out the usurped property.
- It is permissible to exhume the deceased if they were buried in the property of another person without the latter's permission or authorization, provided exhuming the body

does not entail a greater harm such as leaving the corpse without burial or the potential for the corpse to tear apart during the process. Otherwise, it is not permissible; rather based on obligatory precaution, if the usurper was someone other than the deceased and the exhuming results in disrespecting the sanctity of the deceased, the usurper should try to satisfy the owner of the property by any legitimate means (e.g., monetary compensation).

- It is permissible to exhume the corpse if the deceased was buried without being washed, shrouded, or camphorated while it was possible to do so, if it does not result in disrespecting their sanctity. Otherwise, it is problematic to do so (i.e., exhuming should be avoided based on obligatory precaution).
- It is permissible to exhume the corpse if it is determined that washing, shrouding, or camphorating the deceased was done incorrectly, and is therefore invalid, if it does not result in disrespecting their sanctity. Otherwise, it is problematic do so (i.e., exhuming should be avoided based on obligatory precaution).
- It is permissible to exhume the corpse if the deceased was buried in the wrong orientation, such as not facing the direction of the qiblah or in a place other than where they designated in their will, or some other similar circumstance, provided that it does not result in disrespecting their sanctity. Otherwise, it is

problematic to do so (i.e., exhuming should be avoided based on obligatory precaution).
- If the deceased had mentioned in their will that they desired to be transferred to a different place for burial, and doing so would not have resulted in the decay of the corpse or other harm, and yet they were buried in a different place intentionally, ignorantly, or forgetfully, it is obligatory to exhume the corpse and transfer it provided that transferring does not result in the decay of the corpse or other type of harm.

RULING FOR BURIAL AT SEA

If a person dies while at sea (in a ship, a boat, etc.), and it is not possible to bury them on land, albeit by delaying the burial [until reaching the land], they must be washed, shrouded, camphorated, and the funeral prayer must be performed for them. Then they must be placed in a container, such as a bag that should then be tied firmly and sunk in the sea. Moreover, it should be weighed down with something heavy (e.g., rocks) fastened to the legs and then sunk in the sea. The same ruling applies if the deceased is on land but there is a fear that they might be exhumed by the enemy and mutilated.

INCULCATING (TALQIN)

Inculcating the deceased after laying them in the sepulchre (lahd) and before sealing the grave with bricks is among the recommended acts.[42]

---

42. Al-Sayyid al-Yazdi, *Al-urwat-al-wuthqa*, Rulings for burying a deceased.

After Death

Method of inculcating (talqin)

The person performing the inculcation (talqin) should hold the right shoulder of the deceased with their right hand, firmly take the left shoulder with their left hand, place their mouth near the ear of the corpse, and vigorously shake the corpse.

The first method:

Say thrice, "Listen and understand, Oh (name of the deceased, son/daughter of name of their father), God is your lord, and Muhammad is your prophet, and Islam is your religion, and the Quran is your book, and Ali is your divine leader (Imam), and al-Hasan is your divine leader," then mention the names of the rest of the Imams (pbut) and say, "Did you understand (name of the deceased son/daughter, son/daughter of name of their father)?"

Then say, "May God keep you steadfast with the firm saying (i.e., firm beliefs), and may He guide you to the right path, and foster acquaintance between you and your guardians (Ahl al-Bayt [pbut]) in the abode of His mercy. Oh God, expand the ground for him/her on both of his/her sides, ascend his/her spirit (ruh) to You, and direct your proof to him/her. Oh God, [bestow] your pardon, your pardon."

Second Method:

It is reported by Hammad ibn Hariz, that Zurara said, "When you place the deceased in his sepulchre recite Ayat al-Kursi, and firmly take his right shoulder and then say "Oh (name of the deceased) say, 'I accept God as my Lord, and [accept] Muhammad (pbuh&hp) as a prophet, and Ali (p) as an imam,' and then he should say the name of the Imam of his time."[43]

Third method:

The most comprehensive statement of inculcation (talqin) is to say, "Listen Oh (name of the deceased, son/daughter of name of his/her father)" three times, then say,

> Do you hold true to the covenant to which you held when you parted from us? Whereby you testify that there is no god but Allah, He alone, for whom there is no partner; that Muhammad—may Allah bless him and his progeny—is His servant and His messenger and the foremost of all the Prophets and the seal of all the Messengers; that Ali is the Commander of the Faithful and the master of all the successors and an Imam whose obedience Allah has made obligatory on the whole world; that al-Hasan, and al-Hussain, and Ali son of al-Hussain, and Muhammad son of Ali, and Jafar son of Muhammad, and Musa son of Jafar, and Ali son of Musa, and Muhammad son of Ali, and Ali son of Muhammad, and al-Hasan son of Ali, and the one who will rise up, the Proof, al-Mahdi—may God's blessings be upon them all—are Imams of the faithful and Allah's proofs over the whole of creation, and your Imams are Imams of guidance for you and are pious, (Oh name the deceased and their father).
>
> When the two angels who are close [to Allah], come to you as messengers from Allah—the Blessed, the

---

43. Shaykh al-Kulayni, *Al-kafi*, vol. 3, p. 196.

After Death

Exalted—and ask you about your Lord, your Prophet, your religion, your book, your qiblah, and your Imams, then do not fear nor grieve, but say in response to them: Allah is my Lord, Muhammad—may Allah's blessing and peace be upon him and his progeny—is my Prophet, Islam is my religion, the Quran is my book, and the Kabah is my qiblah. The Commander of the Faithful Ali ibn Abi Talib is my Imam, al-Hasan al-Mujtaba is my Imam, al-Hussain the Martyr of Karbala is my Imam, Ali Zayn al-Abidin is my Imam, Muhammad al-Baqir is my Imam, Jafar al-Sadiq is my Imam, Musa al-Kazim is my Imam, Ali al-Rida is my Imam, Muhammad al-Jawad is my Imam, Ali al-Hadi is my Imam, al-Hasan al-Askari is my Imam, and al-Hujjah al-Muntadher is my Imam. All of them—may Allah's blessings be upon them—are my Imams, my masters, my leaders, and my intercessors. I befriend only them and I have hatred only for their enemies in this world and the hereafter. Then know, Oh (name the deceased and their father) Allah, the Blessed, the Exalted, is the best Lord, and Muhammad—may Allah's blessing and peace be upon him and his progeny—is the best messenger, and Ali ibn Abi Talib and his infallible descendants, [together being] the twelve Imams, are the best imams. What Muhammad—may Allah's blessing and peace be upon him and his progeny—brought is true; death is true; the questioning of Munkar and Nakir in the grave is real; the raising [from the graves] is real; the resurrection is real; the Path is real, the Scale is real; the disclosure of the book of deeds is real; Paradise is real; the Fire is real; the Hour is coming, there is no doubt about it; and Allah will raise those who are in the graves.

Then say [to the deceased], "Do you understand (name the deceased)?" It is reported that the deceased would respond by saying "I understand."[44]

Then say [to the deceased] "May God keep you steadfast with the firm saying (i.e., firm beliefs), and may He guide you to the right path, and foster acquaintance between you and your guardians (Ahl al-Bayt [pbut]) in the abode of His mercy. Oh God expand the ground for him/her on both of his/her sides, ascend his/her spirit (ruh) to You, and direct your proof to him/her. Oh God [bestow] your pardon, your pardon."

It is better to inculcate using the Arabic language. If the deceased was not an Arabic speaker, then it is better to inculcate in their language.

When inculcation takes place

Inculcation takes place in the following instances:

- During the throes of death (ihtidar) and when the spirit is close to departing the body
- When the deceased is placed in their grave and after revealing their face
- After the burial and after the funeral procession participants (mourners) depart

---

44. Translation of the inculcations is from Ayatullah al-Sayyid al-Sistani's book, *Islamic Laws*.

Washing after Touching a Corpse (*ghusl mass al-mayyit*)

Who is required to perform ritual washing for touching a corpse?

It is obligatory for a person, irrespective of whether they are sane or insane, a child or an adult, to perform a ritual wash for touching a corpse whether it is of a Muslim or non-Muslim, and even if it is a miscarried or still-born fetus if the spirit had entered into it. However, performing this ritual wash is required only if the corpse is touched after it becomes cool and before it receives the complete wash (i.e., all three washes).

When a ritual wash is not obligatory

Performing a ritual wash for touching a corpse is not obligatory in the following cases:

- If the corpse was washed by a non-Muslim due to lack of availability of a washer of the same gender. In this case, if someone touched the corpse after it was washed, it is not obligatory to perform a wash for touching the corpse.
- It is not obligatory to perform a ritual wash when a corpse is touched after washing it with plain water when water mixed with lote tree leaves (sidr) and camphor were not available.

What is considered a touch that requires washing?

The following instances require washing after touching the corpse:

- Touching with or without wetness

- Touching the inner or outer parts of the corpse with the inner or outer parts of the body
- Touching, irrespective of whether it was voluntary or involuntary

Ruling on touching a corpse that has undergone dry ablution (tayammum) in place of washing (ghusl)

If the corpse has been purified with dry ablution (tayammum) due to washing (ghusl) not being available or possible, it is obligatory to perform a ritual wash for touching it.

Exception from ritual washing for touching a corpse

If a person touches a corpse with their hair or touches the hair of a corpse, they are not required to perform a ritual wash.

Ruling on touching a corpse before it becomes cold

If a person touches a corpse before it becomes cold, they are not required to perform a ritual wash. However, if they touch the deceased with wetness, such that the wetness transfers onto the part it touched, they should purify that part of their body, and the recommended precaution is to do so even if there is no wetness.

Ruling on touching an isolated part of a corpse

There are two cases:

- If the corpse is not fragmented or in pieces, then it is not obligatory to ritually wash for touching part of it, even if it contained bone and flesh, and similarly if the part was separated from the body while it was alive.
- If the corpse is fragmented or in pieces, and a person touches all or most of it, they must perform the ritual wash for touching a corpse.

Ruling on touching a corpse through a barrier

Q: Is it obligatory to perform a wash for touching a corpse if it was through a barrier such as a rubber glove?
A: Ritual washing (ghusl) is not obligatory.

Q: Is it obligatory to perform a ritual wash for touching a corpse covered with a fabric sheet?
A: Ritual washing (ghusl) is not obligatory.

Touching the excretions of a corpse

Q: Is it obligatory to perform a ritual wash for touching the excretions of a corpse, such as the sweat, blood, or similar excretions?
A: Ritual washing (ghusl) is not obligatory.

Acts that are [still] permissible for a person who is required to perform a ritual wash for touching the corpse

It is permissible for a person who is required to perform a ritual wash for touching a corpse to

- enter mosques and holy shrines;
- stay inside a mosque; and

- recite the chapters of the Holy Quran that contain the verses that obligate prostration (*sujud al-tilawah*).[45]

Acts that are not permissible for a person who is required to perform a ritual wash for touching the corpse

The following are not permissible if a person must perform a ritual wash for touching a corpse:

- Touching the writing of the Quran and anything that one must not touch while in the state of impurity (*hadath*)
- Any act of worship that requires being in the state of purity will be deemed invalid unless the person performs a ritual wash for touching the corpse, and the recommended precaution is to perform ablution (wudu) as well if they had done a minor break in the state of purity such as urinating or sleeping prior to performing ghusl.

---

45. The chapters of the Quran that contain the verses that require prostration (sujud) are chapter 32, Surat al-Sajdah; chapter 41, Surat al-Fussilat; chapter 53, Surat al-Najm; and chapter 96, Surat al-Alaq.

Chapter 3

After Burial

The religion of Islam demonstrates a great concern for the deceased after burial, as may be seen in the numerous acts ordained for the believers. Thus, Islam has urged the relatives of the deceased and the believers to fulfill those acts and promised rewards and positive consequences for doing so.

Recommended Acts Performed after Burial

The following are recommended acts to perform after the burial:

- Charity—Giving charity on behalf of the deceased, for it was reported that the Prophet (pbuh&hp) said, "No hour will be harder on the deceased than the first night, so have mercy on your deceased by giving charity."[46]
- Gifted prayer—A prayer that is performed on the night of loneliness and bewilderment (the first night after burying the deceased). The

---

46. Mirza al-Nuri, *Al-mustadrak ala wasail al Shia*, vol. 6, p. 344.

method of performing this prayer is as follows:

- In the first rakah, recite Surat al-Fatihah and Ayat al-Kursi once, and in the second rakah after reciting Surat al-Fatihah, recite Surat al-Qadr ten times. After the salam of the prayer [i.e., completion of the prayer] recite the following supplication, "Oh God! Bless Muhammad and the progeny of Muhammad, and send the reward [of this prayer] to the grave of [name of deceased].[47]
- It is reported that the Prophet (pbuh&hp) said, "No hour will be harder on the deceased than the first night, so have mercy on your deceased by giving charity, and if you are unable [to pay charity] one of you should perform a two rakah prayer in which he recites in the first rakah after Surat al-Fatihah Ayat al-Kursi once, and in the second rakah after Surat al-Fatihah recite Surat al-Qadr ten times, and say after the salam, "Oh God! Bless Muhammad and the progeny of Muhammad, and send the reward [of this prayer] to the grave of [name of deceased].[48] There are other methods reported for performing this prayer.

---

47. There are other methods of performing this prayer in terms of the recitation after Surat al-Fatihah. Please refer to the books of supplications for details.

48. Al-Hurr al-Amili, *Wasail al-Shia*, vol. 8, p. 168.

After Burial

- Visiting the cemetery: The religion of Islam has stressed the importance of visiting graves and explained that it softens the heart, reminds a person of the hereafter, and brings joy to the deceased. It is reported that the Commander of the Faithful (p) said, "Visit your deceased for they become joyous by your visit to them."[49] Also it is reported that Imam al-Sadiq (p) quoted the Commander of the Faithful (p) as saying, "They [deceased ones] are happy and [enjoy] your presence, and feel lonely when you leave."[50] Moreover, visiting graves is a means of attaining forgiveness of sins and fulfillment of needs. It is reported that Imam al-Sadiq (p) said, "Visit your deceased for they become joyous by your visit to them, and any one of you should supplicate to [God] to fulfill your [own] need when visiting the grave of their father and the grave of their mother while[51] they supplicate to God for them.[52] Furthermore, it is narrated that Imam Ali al-Rida (p) said, "One who visits the grave of his [believing] brother, places his hand on the grave, and recites Surat al-Qadr seven times will be safe from the great fear [on the Day of Resurrection]."[53]

---

49. Shaykh al-Kulayni, *Al-kafi*, vol. 3, p. 230.
50. Shaykh al-Kulayni, *Al-kafi*, vol. 3, p. 228.
51. After he supplicates to God for them. This is based on a different copy of the Arabic hadith.
52. Al-Hurr al-Amili, *Wasail al-Shia*, vol. 3, p. 223.
53. Al-Hurr al-Amili, *Wasail al-Shia*, vol. 3, p. 226.

In addition to the general recommendation of reciting the Quran by the graves of the believers, it is recommended to specifically recite Surat al-Fatihah, Surat Ya Sin, Surat al-Ikhlas, Surat al-Falaq, and Surat al-Nas. It also recommended to recite what the Commander of the Faithful Imam Ali (p) is reported to have said, "I heard the Messenger of God (pbuh&hp) say, 'He who recites it when passing by the cemeteries, fifty years of his sins will be forgiven [by God].' At that point the Prophet (pbuh&hp) was asked, 'What if he did not have fifty years of sins?' He replied, 'Then for his parents, brothers [in faith], and the general public of the believers (i.e., they will be forgiven instead if the reciter of this special invocation did not have fifty years of sins).' [This special invocation is]:

> In the Name of God, the Compassionate, the Merciful
>
> Peace be upon the of people of no God but Allah (la ilaha illallah) (i.e., the people who believe in the absolute oneness of God), Oh people of la ilaha illallah, how did you find the [result which came of] la ilaha illallah from la ilaha illallah. Oh, la ilaha illallah, by the sake of la ilaha illallah, forgive those who said la ilaha illallah and resurrect us along with those who said la ilaha illallah.[54]

- Consoling the bereaved—Consoling the bereaved and comforting them before and after the burial of the deceased, although the latter is better. One should refer to what is better based on common view (*urf*). Even being seen by the bereaved is

---

54. Shaykh al-Majlisi, *Bihar al-Anwar*, vol. 99, p. 301

sufficiently consoling to earn the [divine] reward for this act. It is reported that the Holy Prophet (pbuh&hp) said, "He who consoles a griever will be dressed in a garment honoring him."[55] There is no limit to the duration of consolation, but it is better to avoid it if it entails renewing the grief of the bereaved. It is permissible to hold a gathering for consoling the bereaved, and based on some jurists, it should not be more than two or three days. Others consider more than a day as detestable (makruh). However, it is favorable if the gathering is intended for reciting the Quran and supplication to God.

It is better for the consoler to express their condolences to the grieving family and relatives of the deceased and to take into account their feelings and grief by not laughing, bantering, or speaking excessively. Rather, the gathering should encompass exhortation, remembering the hereafter, seeking forgiveness, remembering God, and beseeching Him to bestow His mercy and forgiveness on the deceased.

Further, food should be prepared for the grieving family, and they should not be burdened by subjecting them to customs that compel them to extravagance and waste. Acts of extravagance and waste are a deviance from the holy tradition [of the Prophet (pbuh&hp). Instead, they should limit their mourning activities to

---

55. Al Hurr al-Amili, *Wasail al-Shia*, ch. 46, hadith 1.

reciting the Quran and seeking forgiveness and mercy for the deceased.[56]

Mourning for the Dead

Sadness is an innate state. As such, God has blessed humans to express [through sentiments] what they are unable to express with their tongues and strengthen the human bonds that emanate from love and tenderness. Hence, the Quran mentions the sadness of Jacob for Joseph over their long separation and his weeping that led to the loss of sight, "(Jacob) turned away from them, saying, 'Alas, Joseph is lost!' He wept continuously in his grief until, in suppressing his anger, his eyes turned white. They said, 'You are always remembering Joseph. By Allah, it will either make you sick or you will die.' He replied, 'I complain of my sorrow and grief only to Allah. I about Allah what you do not know .'"[57]

Similarly, it is reported that the Holy Prophet Muhammad (pbuh&hp) wept when his child Ibrahim passed away. He said, "The eyes shed tears and the heart is saddened, however, we will not say what brings the wrath of God."[58] Also, the greatest of all women, Lady Fatimah al-Zahra (p), used to weep over her father's demise. She would bring Hasan and Hussain (pbut) and sit by the grave of her father to mourn. This was also a practice of the Imams of Ahl al-Bayt (pbut) who

---

56. This expresses the tenor of a referendum stamped by the office of His Eminence Ayatullah Sayyid al-Sistani. See the Appendix 1 to this booklet.
57. The Holy Quran 12:84-86.
58. Shaykh al-Kulayni, *Al-kafi*, vol. 3, p. 262.

recommend it. It is reported that Imam Musa al-Kadhim (p) once said, "When a believer dies, the angels weep over him, and so do the parts of the earth on which he used to worship God and the gates of heaven through which his [good] deeds ascended. [His death causes] a void that nothing can fill because the believers are the fortresses of Islam, like the protecting wall that is built around a town [for protecting it]."[59]

In view of the differences in relations and filial connections and the nature of certain special relationships, such as between spouses, Islam has legislated for only[60] the wife to observe a waiting period, which God refers to in the Holy Quran, "The wives of those of you who die have to wait for a period of four months and ten days."[61]

During the waiting period, the wife is required to observe a state of mourning (*hidad*) by avoiding all that is considered an adornment to the body or clothes based on the custom of society. Therefore, she must avoid wearing eyeliner (*kohl*), makeup, and perfume, as well as hair dye, gold, silver, and other types of jewelry. In general, she must avoid anything that is considered an adornment based on the social customs in her locality (this varies according to different times, places, and traditions).

---

59. Al-Hurr al-Amili, *Wasail al-Shia*, vol. 3, p. 283.
60. Islam has legislated for the wife only and not the mother, daughter, sister, or other female relative.
61. The Holy Quran 2:234.

Conclusion

We have reached the end of this booklet on the rulings of death and burial hoping that it is free from any deficiency, error, or omission. We beseech God to pardon our shortcomings given that absolute perfection is His alone. We also hope that our respected readers will point out anything that needs correction or updating. We pray to God that He accepts this effort and grants all the believers success in reaching a good final ending after living a happy life filled with knowledge, faith, and good deeds, "On the day when every soul will see its good and bad deeds right before its very eyes."[62] Truly, success can be achieved only from God.

---

62. The Holy Quran 3:30.

Appendix 1

The Islamic etiquette of offering condolences to those who lost their loved one according to Grand Ayatullah Sayyid al-Sistani's opinion

In the name of God, the Exalted

Offering condolences to the bereaved, although it is a Prophetic practice highly emphasized and highly rewarded, according to the narrations, it is sufficient for the bereaved to see the condoler, for it is reported in the holy tradition, "It is sufficient in condoling that the bereaved person sees you." Moreover, it is permissible to attend the funeral, although it has been said [by some scholars] that it is detestable to sit for more than a day unless it is for the purpose of reciting the Quran and supplicating to God. Nevertheless, it is necessary to observe the etiquette of condolence. Therefore, it is not good to burden the family and relatives of the deceased and impose hardship upon them, for this contradicts the manners of giving condolence. Instead, consider helping and supporting them however possible. It is recommended to send them food, as it serves as a means of honoring them and lessening their distress. It is also detestable to take a meal from their food with them. It is reported that Imam al-Sadiq said, "Eating from the bereaving family is a practice of the people of ignorance [during the Age of Ignorance before the advent of Islam]." Some

Appendix 1

scholars stated that this pertains to eating from what the bereaving family has prepared and not what has been prepared by their relatives and neighbors. In addition, mourners must observe Islamic rulings when giving condolence to the bereaved by avoiding any form of disposing of their possessions without their consent or using their things extravagantly or wastefully, and this means one should observe piety. Also, there is a reminder and lessons to be derived from remembering death. The believer must remember that he will soon follow the deceased. Thus, he should take precaution in matters of religion. One must not allow negligence to distort this honorable practice and defeat its purpose of lessening the burden on the bereaved and honoring them. Otherwise, it will lead to diminishing rewards, the removal of blessings, and cause division, and God knows best.

11/Jumada al-Thani/1428 AH
Seal of Sayyid al-Sistani's office in Najaf, Iraq

Appendix 1

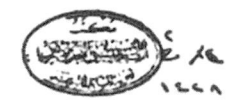

بسم الله تعالى :

ان تعزية المصاب وان كانت مسنّة مؤكدة بل فيها أجر عظيم وثواب جسيم كما نطقت بفضلها الأخبار إلا أنه يكفي فيها رؤية صاحب المصيبة كما ورد في الحديث وكفاك من التعزية أنه يرى صاحب المصيبة) وتجهيز المجالس فيها ولكن تبديل بكرهه ما زاد على يوم واحد إلا أن تكون المجالس متعقد لقراءة القرآن والدعاء.

وينبغي مع ذلك مراعاة آداب التعزية فلا يحسن التثقيل على أهل الميت وذويهم وازعاجهم بل ان ذلك فيه فيه التسلية لهم والمواساة معهم . بل يراعى بالتخفيف منهم وإمانتهم ما امكن .

وقد ورد استحباب ارسال الطعام اليهم . وكأنه لدفع الغم وعنهم وتكريم لهم، كما ورد ذكرا هدا الأذكى عنصرهم . ففي الحديث . عن الصادق عليه السلام : الاكل عند اهل المصيبة من عمل أهل الجاهلية) . وذكر بعض الفقهاء أنه يختص بما كان من عندهم لما يهدى اليهم من الأقرباء وابيداء على السنّة المذكورة .

كما يجب مراعاة العزين للمحدد الشرعية في تعزيتهم وعدم ورودهم على أهل الميت سوى اجتناب العادات المضرة بهم والتصرف في أموالهم بغير رضا صاحب الشأن والأسراف فيها ناه هذا المقام أحق بمراعاة ، فتصرف فيه ناه في ذكر الموت عظة لمن يتعظ معبرة لمن يعتبر وعلى الذمة أن يتذكر أنه لا دعى بهم من ترتيب شيئاً ما لدينه ما بناه ، لا قُدرت الغفلة الى تحريف هذه السنة السنّه عما أُريد بها سواه التخفيف عن أهل الميت والتكرم لهم الخلاف ذلك فيحبط بذلك الأجر وتذرك البركة وتجب الغربة . والله العالم.

Appendix 2

New rulings regarding washing, shrouding, and burial of a deceased person in a situation that involves infectious diseases (e.g., COVID-19)

Question: Would the disapproval of leaving a dying person alone be lifted in a coronavirus infected case?
Answer: If someone fears they will suffer harm due to the fulfillment of given act, then what was obligatory (wajib) no longer remains obligatory, and what was recommended (mustahabb) or disliked (makruh) must be avoided. In cases other than these, the act can be performed.

Question: With reference to Ruling 664 in the *Tawdih al-masail jami* book, would it be recommended (mustahabb) to close the eyes and mouth of a dead body that is infected with the coronavirus?
Answer: It is as answered earlier—if someone fears they will suffer harm due to the fulfillment of given act, then what was obligatory (wajib) no longer remains obligatory, and what was recommended (mustahabb) or disliked (makruh) must be avoided. In cases other than these, the act can be performed.

Question: With reference to Ruling 706 in *Tawdih al-masail jami*, if performing ghusl on a dead body that has been infected with the coronavirus poses a risk for the person doing the washing, can tayammum be

performed instead?
Answer: Yes, if there are no means for performing ghusl without risk, then tayammum must be performed.

Question: If it is harmful to perform tayammum on a dead body infected with the coronavirus, either with the hands of the person performing the tayammum or with the hands of the dead body, how would tayammum be performed?
Answer: Tayammum on a dead body must be performed by the hands of the one performing tayammum (i.e., the one performing the rituals of death and burial), and in case performing it without wearing gloves poses a risk, then there is no problem in wearing gloves.

Question: If performing tayammum on a dead body becomes obligatory (wajib) but there is a high risk of contracting the coronavirus, is it permitted to bury the dead body without ghusl and tayammum?
Answer: If there is fear of harm in performing ghusl or tayammum, then the dead body must be buried without ghusl and tayammum.

Question: With reference to Ruling 728 in *Tawdih al-masail jami*, if it is not possible to apply obligatory (wajib) camphor to a dead body that is infected with the coronavirus, is it permissible to leave it without camphorating, and is there any replacement act?
Answer: In case of fear of harm, it is not required, and there is no replacement.

Appendix 2

Question: With reference to Rulings 755 and 757 in *Tawdih al-masail jami*, is it allowed to bury a dead body infected with the coronavirus in a coffin?
Answer: There is no problem in placing the dead body in a coffin. If the coffin is buried in the ground, then, of course, the dead body must be laid on its right side in a way that the front of the body faces the qiblah.

Question: With reference to Ruling 756, in *Tawdih al-masail jami*, if based on obligatory precaution it is not allowed to keep a dead body in cold storage, then is it permissible to do so if the body is infected with the coronavirus until it is safe for burial?
Answer: If it is required to keep the body in cold storage for a relatively long period of time so that the obligatory (wajib) acts of burial can be performed, then there is no problem; in fact, in such a case, it is necessary [to keep it in cold storage].

Question: With reference to Ruling 758 in *Tawdih al-masail jami*, if someone dies on a ship, the burial must be delayed until the ship reaches land. In such a case, should the burial be delayed until the infection is controlled, so that the obligatory (wajib) acts of burial can be performed on a dead body infected with the coronavirus?
Answer: There is no problem [in delaying the burial] if the dead body does not decompose and there is no issue with it staying in cold storage.

Question: What should be our duty towards non-Muslims who are affected with the coronavirus locally and globally?

Answer: Helping them to recover and get better is an admirable thing to do.

Question: What is the ruling on washing, shrouding, and burying the body of a dead person if the cause of death is an infectious virus (or other contagious pathogen) that requires caution and avoidance according to the religious edicts of his eminence Ayatullah al-Sayyid al-Sistani (may God prolong his life)?

Answer: Any act that poses harm to the person who undertakes the preparation of the deceased [under such circumstances] is revoked. However, if it is possible to perform tayammum on the deceased, albeit wearing gloves, and to shroud the body, even if with a plastic cover, it must be done. Thereafter, the funeral prayer and burial should be performed as required.

Question: Does the obligation of performing the ritual wash (ghusl) and dry ablution (tayammum) on a deceased become revoked if the cause of death is an infectious virus (or other contagious pathogen) and fear of transmission of the infection exists [for those performing the ritual acts]?

Answer: If it is not possible to perform the ritual wash on the deceased due to fear of transmission of infection, even when wearing special [protective] clothing meant for dealing with infected individuals, one must resort to dry ablution (tayammum), even if by using medical gloves. If that is not possible either, the obligation is revoked. Hence, the deceased should be buried without a ritual wash or dry ablution.

Appendix 2

Question: Does the obligation of shrouding (takfin) the deceased become revoked if the cause of death is an infectious virus (or other contagious pathogen), just as the ritual wash (ghusl) and dry ablution (tayammum) become revoked due to fear of transmission of the infection? What about the funeral prayer?
Answer: It is necessary to shroud the deceased with three garments if possible, even if it is done over insulating plastic. Moreover, prayer must be performed for them. Thereafter, the deceased can be placed in a box and buried. However, if possible, they must be placed on their right side facing the direction of the qiblah.

Question: Is it obligatory to perform a ritual wash (ghusl) on the body of a person who died due to COVID-19 or is it enough to perform dry ablution (tayammum)? What if the health authorities do not allow dry ablution (tayammum) given medical staff place the deceased in a special bag with preservatives and prohibit the bag from being opened before burial?
Answer: If performing a ritual bath (ghusl) on the dead body is not possible due to a risk of transmission, then dry ablution (tayammum) must be performed on it by the hands of a living person, even if it is performed wearing gloves. If tayammum is not possible either [due to the high risk of disease communication], or the health authorities prohibit it, the dead body must be buried without ghusl or tayammum.

Question: Is shrouding the dead body with three garments obligatory? What if the health authorities prohibit the sealed plastic that is wrapped over the body from being opened, is it permissible to shroud the body over the plastic?

Answer: It is necessary to shroud the deceased with three garments if possible, even if it is done over a sealed plastic cover. If it is not possible to shroud the body with all three garments then it must be shrouded with what is feasible, such as the full wrapping or izar that covers the entire body.

Question: Cadavers infected with contagious pathogens (e.g., coronavirus) are often cremated in some non-Muslim countries. Is it permissible to cremate a Muslim's body? Should the family of the deceased refrain from it if they have a choice?

Answer: It is not permissible to cremate the dead body of a Muslim, and the family, relatives, or anyone else must refrain from it and insist on burying the deceased according to Islamic laws.

Appendix 2

The Q & As were generated from the following documents:

بسم الله الرحمن الرحیم

علیکم السلام ورحمة الله وبرکاته

ج ١ : اول : دعا وتضرع در درگاه خداوند متعال جهت رفع این بلا از امکان، امید است ادعیه مؤمنین مورد اجابت حضرت حق تعالی واقع گردد . دوم : رعایت اصول بهداشتی در حد امکان . سوم : سعی و کلک دیگران جهت در امان بودن از این بیماری ، و در صورت امکان رسیدگی به مبتلایان به آن اجر اخروی انشاء الله البته صفیا مراتب دوا و مراجعه در موارد و مجالاتی واجب خواهد بود .

ج ٢ : در هر جایی که منظر علم گیری از انتشار بیماری با دیده اگر در تجمعات ممنوع است باید این جمع حتی گرفته شود ، و در صورت عدم منع با رعایت اصول بهداشتی اشکال ندارد . البته هر متخصصی که حفظ آن را دارد که در اثر حضور در تجمعات مردم مبتلا به این بیماری شود و آسیب شدیدی ببیند و یا معرض مرگ شود باید از این امر اجتناب کند .

ج ٣ : با فاصله بیشتر و ماندن آن فی مانع است ، و اما اگر فاصله بین صفها رکعت ارتان در ملک صف در این جای بای صف جلو و جای مجمعی صف عقب در متر و یا ماندن آن باشد انعقاد جماعت محل اشکال است .

ج ٤ : اشکال ندارد ولی باید در هر مورد با او اجابت آمین بنماید و موجب هتک حرمت طرف نشود .

ج ٥ : رعایت اصول بهداشتی نسبت به عذر شخص در صورتی که حفظ ابتلا دم و ویروس را دشنه به استفاده اعمال حتی بعد کردن عرض اسلام منجر به مرگ ، و یا آسیب شدید شود حتما لازم است . و جنانچه رعایت نکند و آخر ما احتمالا جدا به محقق شود مرتکب معذور نخواهد بود . و اگر شخصی مبتلا به این بیماری است و در نیاس دیگران اصول بهداشتی را رعایت نکند و عوض بی اطلاع باشد صاحب من آسیبی است که راو وارد و به نه شود ، و اگر منجر به مرگ شود دیت ثابت خواهد بود . واگر کار کاری است که از راه کار در نتواند کند بعید نیست در دوران معالجه و عجز از بکار اجره المثل در ضامن باشد .

ج ٦ : جواب سؤال (٥) ملاحظه شود .

ج ٨ و ٧ و ٩ و ١٠ : با عوض حضر آخر و اجابت ماسط و شود و آجه مستحب و با مکر و ه است . در صورت عوض صفر شدید لازم الاجتناب است ، و در غیر این صورت می توان آن را انجام داد .

ج ١١ : بله اگر غسلهای برای غسل دادن در خطر باشد غوبت به تیمم می رسد .

ج ١٢ : تیمم میت باید با دستهای تیمم دهنده باشد ، و در صورتی که در دستکش خطر داشت بی استبداد دستکش

ج ١٣ : در عرض خوف حضر از اجرای غسل و تیمم مالقیا میت بدون غسل و تیمم دفن و به شود .

ج ١٤ : در صورت خوف حضر ماسط وسود و جایگزین ندارد .

ج ١٥ : کفن استخوانی که در تابوت اشکال ندارد ، اگر ثابت در زمین دفن شود ، البته باید میت را در تابوت به جهتی راست خوابانند به تخصی که جلوی بدن او رو به قبله باشد .

ج ١٦ : اگر تیمیز بودن مست از خو ولجب نگهداشته اود در هر غذای برای مدت نسبتا طولانی اقتضا به استفاده اشکال ندارد بلکه لازم است . ج ١٧ : در زمانی که جسد را فاسد می شود و بودن او در هر غذای جا مانع استفاده اشکال ندارد .

ج ١٨ : کلک در آنات در هر زمان دعوی وعالم شان کار پسندیده ای است .

ج ١٩ : باید معتقد بود که تمام اخبار از مصائب و بلایا واقع و شود و حکمتی دارد هر چند ما از آن آگاه نیستیم .

ج ٢٠ : به خواندن قرآن مجید و ادعیه وارده از اهل بیت عصمت و طهارت علیهم السلام توصیه می شود .

اسأل الله عز جمعه کل صدور بلاد و السلام علیکم و علی سائر المؤمنین للمؤمنات ورحمة الله و برکاته .

١٣ رجب ١٤٤١ ه‍

Appendix 2

بِسْمِ اللهِ الرَّحْمَنِ الرَّحِيمِ

مكتب سماحة المرجع الاعلى السيد السيستاني حفظه الله تعالى

السلام عليكم ورحمة الله وبركاته

لا يخفى عليكم ما يتعرض له الناس في هذه الايام بسبب (وباء فيروس كورونا) والكادر الطبي والتمريضي والمتطوعون في المستشفيات والمراكز الطبية التي تتعامل مع المصابين بهذا الفيروس او من يشك في اصابتهم به يخاطرون بصحتهم وربما بحياتهم فيما يقومون به، لأنهم عرضة لانتقال العدوى اليهم، ما هي كلمة المرجعية الدينية لهم؟ افيدونا مشكورين.

بسم الله الرحمن الرحيم

ان علاج المرضى ورعايتهم والقيام بشؤونهم واجب كفائي على كل المؤهلين لأداء هذه المهام من الاطباء وكادر التمريضي وغيرهم، وكذلك يجب على السلطات المعنية ان توفر لهم كل المستلزمات الضرورية لحمايتهم من مخاطر الاصابة بالمرض، ولا عذر لها في التخلف عن ذلك.

ولا شك في ان ما يقوم به هؤلاء الاعزة - بالرغم من كل التحديات - عمل عظيم وجهد يقدّر بثمن، ولعل يقارب في الاهمية مرابطة المقاتلين الابطال في الثغور دفاعاً عن البلاد أعلم.

ومن المؤكد ان الله تبارك وتعالى يقدّر لهم جهودهم في الدنيا ويثيبهم عليها في الآخرة، بل يرجى لمن تضحي بحياته منهم في هذا السبيل ان يثبت له اجر الشهيد ومكانته في يوم الحساب.

وانا اذ نقدم لهم جزيل الشكر و بالغ التقدير على عملهم الاسمى الجليل ندعو الله العلي القدير ان يحميهم ويحفظهم ويبعد عنهم كل سوء، انه سميع مجيب.

٢١/رجب/١٤٤١

Appendix 2

بسم الله الرحمن الرحيم

مكتب سماحة المرجع الديني الأعلى السيد علي السيستاني دام ظله

السلام عليكم ورحمة الله وبركاته

في هذه الايام العصيبة التي ابتلي فيها العراقيون كغيرهم بوباء (كورونا) وفي ظل تعطل الكثير من الاعمال وتحديد حركة المواطنين بل ومنع التجول في غالب المناطق اضيف الى العوائل الفقيرة في المجتمع ـ وما أكثرها ـ عوائل كثيرة اخرى كانت تعتمد في استحصال قوتها في كل يوم على ما يكسبه احد افرادها من خلال عمله اليومي، وقد انسد عليها هذا الباب واصبحت الغالبية العظمى منهم في وضع صعب حيث لا يتيسر لهم توفير الحد الادنى مما يلزمهم من الطعام ونحوها من المستلزمات المعيشية. فما هو توجيه المرجعية الدينية في هذا الصدد؟ افيدونا مشكورين.

جمع من المؤمنين

بسم الله الرحمن الرحيم

ان توفير الحاجات الاساسية للعوائل المتضررة من الاوضاع الراهنة هو بالدرجة الاساس من مسؤولية الجهات الحكومية المعنية ولكن في ظل عدم الاهتمام الكافي منها بذلك لا مناص من التوجه الى سائر الاطراف القادرة على المساهمة في هذا الامر المهم الذي هو من افضل الخيرات والقربات.

والعمل بما يفي بالمقصود يتطلب تعاوناً وتقدّم من عدة اطراف:

1 ـ اهل الخير من المتمكنين مالياً بان يساهموا بما يتيسّر لهم في هذا المجال، ويمكنهم احتساب ما يدفعونه من الحقوق الشرعية مع رعاية الضوابط المقررة في كيفية صرفها وتوزيعها.

2 ـ التجار ممن تتوفر لديهم المواد الغذائية ونحوها بان يعرضوها للبيع ولا يرفعوا من اسعارها بل ينبغي ان تكون مدعومة.

3 ـ مجاميع من الشباب الغيارى يتطوعون للتعرّف على العوائل المتعففة وايصال المواد المحضّرة لهم مع بعد التنسيق في حركتهم مع الجهات الرسمية في ظل منع التجول الساري في معظم المناطق، و لا بد من ان يتخذوا كافة الاجراءات الاحترازية للئلا تنتقل العدوى اليهم لا سمح الله.

وينبغي لاصحاب المواكب الحسينية الكرام ـ الذين كان لهم دور مشرّف في رفد المقاتلين الابطال بكل ما يحتاجونه في ايام الحرب مع داعش ـ ان يستعيدوا نشاطهم باتجاه دعم واسناد العوائل المتضررة في الوقت الراهن مع رعاية ما تقدم آنفاً.

نسأل الله العلي القدير ان يأخذ بأيدي الجميع الى ما فيه الخير والصلاح وليدفع هذا البلاء عن البلاد، انه رؤوف رحيم. والسلام عليكم ورحمة الله وبركاته.

٥٠ رجب ١٤٤١

Appendix 2

بسم الله الرحمن الرحيم

مكتب سماحة المرجع الديني الأعلى السيد السيستاني دام ظله
السلام عليكم ورحمة الله وبركاته

يتسع انتشار فيروس كورونا في الكثير من بلدان العالم وتزداد اعداد المصابين به يوماً بعد يوم وقد علمنا بموقف المرجعية الدينية العليا من (وجوب إتّباع التعليمات الصادرة من الجهات المعنيّة بهدف الحدّ من انتشار هذا الوباء الخطير، ومن ذلك المنع من اقامة التجمعات والحضور فيها لأيّ هدف كان) ولدينا عدد من الأسئلة نتوجه الى سيدنا المرجع الأعلى دام ظله بطلب الاجابة عليها:

١- هل يلزم التجنب عن المماسة مع الآخرين ـ بالمصافحة أو المعانقة او التقبيل أو ما ماثل ذلك، وهل تجوز المخالطة معهم من دون اتخاذ الإجراءات الاحتياطية كلبس الكمامات الطبية ونحو ذلك؟

٢- المصاب بهذا المرض ومن عنده بعض العلامات المحتملة للإصابة به هل يجوز له أن يختلط بالآخرين ممن لا يعلمون بحاله، واذا قام بذلك وانتقلت العدوى اليهم فما هو مسؤوليته تجاههم؟

٣- من يقدم الى البلد من بلد آخر انتشر فيه الفيروس او اختلط ببعض المصابين به هل يجب عليه أن يلتزم بالحجر المنزلي او عرض نفسه للفحص الطبي للتأكد من سلامته من هذا المرض أو لا؟

٤- هل يجوز صرف الحقوق الشرعية من الزكاة والخمس في توفير الادوات الضرورية للحماية من انتقال العدوى من المصابين كالكفوف والكمامات الطبية والمواد المنظفة والمعقمة وكذلك الادوية والمستلزمات الأخرى مما تمس الحاجة اليها في مكافحة هذا الوباء.

٥- بماذا تنصحون المؤمنين في هذا الظرف العصيب الذي يواجهون فيه هذا الوباء الخطير؟

جمع من المؤمنين

بسم الله الرحمن الرحيم

١- من يحتمل أن تنتقل اليه العدوى نتيجة للمماسة او الاختلاط يستضر بصرر بليغاً ولو دون الموت يلزمه التجنب عن ذلك ـ الى اتخاذ الإجراءات الاحترازية اللازمة ـ كالتعقيم واستخدام الكمامة المناسبة والكفوف الطبية ـ بحيث يطمئن معها بعدم اصابته بالمرض، واذا لم يتقيّد برعاية ماذكر واصاب ماكان بإمكانه ألّا يكون معذوراً في ذلك شرعاً.

٢- لا يجوز له أن يختلط بالآخرين بحيث يحتمل انتقال العدوى اليهم، ولو فعل وتسبب في اصابة غيره ممن لا يعلم بحاله كان ضامناً لما لحق به من الضرر، ولدومات جرّاء والاصابة لزمته ديته.

٣- ثم يلزم ذلك مراعاة التعليمات الصادرة من الجهات ذات العلاقة بعد الثأن. الرسمية.

٤- لا مانع من أن تصرف من سهم سبيل الله من الزكاة ومن سهم الامام (ع) من الخمس في ذلك مع رعاية الضوابط.

٥- ننصح المؤمنين الكرام (اعظم الله تعالى) بأمور: أ- الالتجاء الى الله عزّوجل والتضرع اليه لدفع هذا البلاء، والاكثار من الاعمال الصالحة كالتصدق على الفقراء واعانة الضعفاء وقراءة القرآن المجيد والدعاء المأثور عن النبي (ص) واهل بيته اطهار عليهم السلام. ب- الحذر الاولي بجميع هذا الوباء من غيره مع اضطراب الأخذ بأتم اسباب الوقاية والعلاج منه وفق مايقرره اهل الاختصاص بعيداً عن الاساليب غير العلمية. ج- العمل على توعية الآخرين بمخاطر الاستهانة بهذا الفيروس وحثهم على الالتزام بالتوجيهات الصادرة من الجهات المعنية وعدم التخلف عنها. د- مساعدة العوائل المتضررة من الوضع الراهن بسبب تعطّل الاعمال وتفشي البطالة. هـ- رعاية المصابين بغض النظر عن انتمائهم الديني للترغيب والسعي في التخفيف عنهم واعانتهم فيما يحتاجون اليه.

ابعد الله عن الجميع كلّ سوء وبلاء والسلام عليكم ورحمة الله وبركاته ٢٧/رجب/ ١٤٤١هـ

Appendix 2

بسم الله الرحمن الرحيم

مكتب سماحة المرجع الديني الأعلى السيد السيستاني دام ظله

السلام عليكم ورحمة الله وبركاته

يرجى الاجابة على الأسئلة التالية حول المتوفين بوباء (كورونا):

١) المسلم المتوفى بهذا المرض هل يجب تغسيله كغيره من الاموات او انه يكفي أن ييمم؟ وماذا اذا لم تسمح السلطات بإجراء التيمم عليه أيضاً حيث تضعه الملاكات الطبية في كيس خاص مع مواد كيمياوية حافظة وتمنع من فتح الكيس قبل الدفن؟

٢) اذا لم يتيسر تحنيطه بأمساس مساجده السبعة بالكافور فهل له بديل يعمل به؟

٣) هل يجب تكفينه بالأثواب الثلاثة؟ وماذا اذا لم تسمح السلطات بفتح الكيس الذي يغطى به ليكفن بها؟

٤) في بعض البلدان غير الاسلامية يتم حرق جثث المتوفين بالكورونا فهل يجوز السماح بحرق جثة المسلم أم يجب على أهله الممانعة منه اذا وسعهم ذلك؟

٥) ما حكم وضعه في صندوق (تابوت) ودفن الصندوق في الارض؟

٦) يقول أهل الاختصاص انه يمكن دفن المتوفى بالكورونا في اماكن الدفن المتعارف عليها في البلد ولا حاجة الى اجراء استثنائي لذلك من ناحية عمق القبر او غيره، لأن الفيروس يعتمد على الخلايا الحية في بقائه، وبعد موت المصاب يستمر الفيروس في البقاء لمدة قد تمتد لساعات ولكن لا يمتلك طريقة للخروج من الجسد ثم يتلف. فيكفي اتخاذ الاحتياطات الطبية في عملية نقل جثة المصاب ودفنه من ارتداء القفازات الطبية والكمامات العازلة ونحو ذلك، ولا خوف بعد الدفن من انتقال العدوى الى الغير. وفي ضوء ذلك ما حكم الممانعة من دفن المتوفى بالكورونا في المقابر العامة في البلد - ولو في مكان معزول عن سائر القبور - خلافاً لوصيته او رغبة ذويه؟ أجيبونا مشكورين.

بسم الله الرحمن الرحيم

١- اذا لم يتيسّر تغسيله لخوف انتقال العدوى منه فإن تيسّر أن ييمم ببدائحي ولو بوضع استخدام للقفازات يتعين ذلك، ولو لم يتيسّر ايضاً أو منعت منه السلطات المختصة دفن بلا غسل ولا تيمم .

٢- يسقط التحنيط عندئذٍ ولا بدل له .

٣- يجب تكفينه بالاثواب الثلاثة ولم من حنوط الكفن، ولو لم يتيسّر تكفينه جميعاً فليكفن بالمتيسّر منها كالازار الذي يغطي تمام البدن .

٤- لا يجوز حرق جثمان الميت المسلم ويجب على ذويه وغيرهم الممانعة من ذلك بالاصرار على دفنه وفق ما يجب في الشرع الحنيف .

٥- يجوز ذلك، ولكن لا بد مع الامكان من أن يوضع في الصندوق على الجانب الأيمن وجهه الى القبلة كما لو كان يوضع على التراب .

٦- لا يجوز في مفروض السؤال الممانعة من دفنه في المقابر العامة، وعلى السلطات المعنية تسهيل الأمر في ذلك . والله العالي .

٣/ شعبان ١٤٤١هـ

Glossary

adil (عَادِل). Just.

ashnan (أَشْنَان). A tree from the Chenopodiaceous subfamily that grows in sandy soil; it (or its dried powder) is commonly used for washing clothes and hands.

awlia (أَوْلِيَاء). Close servants of Allah and successors of His messenger—the twelve Imams (p).

dua (دُعَاء). Supplication.

dafn (دَفْن). Burial.

fahwa (فَحْوَى). Reasonable appropriate usage based on tacit agreement.

fatwa (فَتْوَى). Religious verdict from a jurist of emulation (marja).

ghusl (غُسْل). Ritual wash or major ablution performed by washing (with water only) the whole body as prescribed by Islamic rules—either by washing every body part in stages from the head to the neck on the right side of the body and then the left (as one would have to do in a shower) or by immersing the whole body in water at once (as one could do in a river).

ghusl mass al-mayyit (غُسْل مَسّ الْمَيِّت). Ritual wash after touching a corpse.

hadath (حَدَث). State of ritual impurity.

hajj (حَجّ). Pilgrimage that must be performed once in a lifetime.

haram (حَرَام). Forbidden, prohibited, not allowed.

hidad (حِدَاد). State of mourning for the widow during which time she must avoid adornment.

ibaha (إِبَاحَة). Permissibility of use.

ihram (إِحْرَام). State of consecration that a pilgrim assumes during hajj. The plain clothing worn by a pilgrim during hajj.

ihtidar (اِحْتِضَار). Time of death.

ihtiyat wajib (اِحْتِيَاط وَاجِب). Precautionary obligation. This means a precautionary measure in which the follower must either follow the opinion of their jurist or follow the opinion of the second-most learned jurist on that issue.

irtimasi (اِرْتِمَاسِي). Immersive ritual wash.

izar (إِزَار). Full cover for shrouding the body of the deceased.

janabah (جَنَابَة). The state of ritual impurity caused by discharge of semen or sexual intercourse.

jaridah (جَرِيْدَة). A twig buried with the body of the deceased.

kafur (كَافُوْر). Camphor.

kalimat al-faraj (كَلِمَاتُ الفَرَج). Words of deliverance to repeat to a dying person.

khums (خُمْس). Religious dues of one fifth of annual acquired wealth.

kohl (كُحل). Eyeliner.

kurr (كُرّ). A large amount of water, which has a minimum of approximately 384 liters.

lahd (لَحْد). A sepulchre within the grave.

lubbah (لُبَّة). The manubrium or bone just above the chest.

Glossary

makruh (مَكْرُوْه). A jurisprudential term meaning detestable or abominable. Although such acts are not forbidden or subject to punishment, refraining from such acts will be rewarded.

mawt (مَوْت). Death.

mithqal (مِثْقَال). A standardized amount, usually by weight.

mithqal sayrafi (مِثْقَال صَيْرَفِي). A weight that is well-known in the market; especially to the goldsmith (.16 ounce/ 4.64 grams).

mizar (مِئْزَر). Loin cloth used in shrouding a body.

mubah (عَادِل). Permissible.

mudhaf (مُضَاف). Mixed—used to describe water that has become mixed with something else such that it can no longer be considered plain water.

mumayyiz (مُمَيِّز). A child who is near the age of a baligh. They are capable of rational actions and knowing the difference between haram and halal. Some of their religious duties are accepted by God, like following a jurist, undertaking something, and buying and selling.

mustahabb (مُسْتَحَب). A jurisprudential term meaning recommended under Islamic law. It is better to perform recommended actions than not to perform them, but they are not compulsory.

mutanajjis (مُتَنَجِّس). An item that is not normally najis (impure) but has become najis by secondary causes, as opposed to *ayn najis* (essentially impure).

mutlaq (مُطْلَق). Plain, unmixed.

najasah (نَجَاسَة). Something that is najis.

najis (نَجِس). Ritually impure.

Glossary

niyyah (نِيَّة). Intention.

niyyah al-raja (نِيَّةُ الرَّجَاء). The intention of hoping that an act is ordained by God.

obligatory precaution (اِحْتِيَاط وُجُوْبِي). This means a precautionary measure in which the follower must either follow the opinion of their jurist or follow the opinion of the second-most learned jurist on that issue.

qada al-salat (قَضَاءُ الصَّلاة). Make up prayer.

qada al-siam (قَضَاءُ الصِّيَام). Make up fasts.

qalil (قَلِيْل). Little—usually used to describe an amount of water for the purposes of purification.

qamis (قَمِيْص). A tunic or long shirt used to shroud a body.

qiblah (قِبْلَة). The direction towards the Holy Kabah in Mecca.

qurbah (قُرْبَة). Nearness.

rahn (رَهْن). Mortgage.

raghwat al-sidr (رَغْوَةُ السِّدْر). The foamy surface of sidr water.

recommended precaution (اِحْتِيَاط اسْتِحْبَابِي). A precautionary act that may be abandoned by a person because it is only recommended and not obligatory.

ruh (رُوْح). Soul.

sadaqah (صَدَقَة). Charity.

salat al-mayyit (صَلاةُ الْمَيِّت). Funeral prayer.

salawat (صَلَوَات). Invoking blessings on Prophet Muhammad and his holy progeny.

Glossary

shahadatayn (شَهَادَتَيْن). Profession of faith that there is no god but Allah and that Muhammad is His messenger.

sidr (سِدْر). Lote tree leaves.

sujud (سُجُوْد). Prostration.

sujud al-tilawah (سُجُوْد التِّلاوَة). Verses in the Quran that obligate prostration.

tahir (طَاهِر). Ritually pure.

tahnit (تَحْنِيْط). Camphorating the body.

takbir (تَكْبِيْر). Recitation of Allahu akbar.

takfin (تَكْفِيْن). Shrouding the body.

talqin (تَلْقِيْن). Inculcation of the testimonies of faith.

tartibi (تَرْتِيْب). Sequential method of ritually washing the body.

tayammum (تَيَمُّم). A substitute for wudu and ghusl when water is unavailable. It is done by striking the hands on the earth and then wiping the forehead and the hands. With the inside of the left hand, wipe the outside of the right hand. Then with the inside of the right hand, wipe the outside of the left hand. For ghusl, strike the ground and wipe in the same way again.

urf (عُرْف). Common view.

wafat (وَفَاة). A term indicating the return of the soul to God.

wajib (وَاجِب). Obligatory.

wajib ayni (وَاجِب عَيْنِي). An essential obligation (i.e., it is obligatory on everyone who meets the criteria).

wajib kifai (وَاجِب كِفَائِي). An action that is only obligatory if it is not performed by others.

Glossary

wali (وَلِيّ). Guardian. Someone who is entrusted to manage someone else's affairs, especially those of a minor, a child, or Islamic society, all under Islamic laws. He shall be one of these three persons: the father, the paternal grandfather, or the current legitimate jurist. There is a hierarchy of guardianship for the deceased.

waqf (وَقْف). A place endowed for a specific purpose.

wasi (وَصِيّ). Executor. The person(s) appointed by the testator [or named in a will], to execute, administer, and distribute the estate in accordance with the will. This person is also known as an administrator or a trustee.

wudu (وُضُوء). Ritual ablution.

Other publications from I.M.A.M.

Available for purchase online

- ❖ Youth: Advice from Grand Ayatullah Sayyid Ali al-Husseini al-Sistani
  Also available in Arabic, Farsi, and Urdu
- ❖ Islamic Laws of the Will by Grand Ayatullah Sayyid Ali al-Husseini al-Sistani
- ❖ Islamic Laws of Expiation by Grand Ayatullah Sayyid Ali al-Husseini al-Sistani
- ❖ Islamic Laws of Food & Drink by Grand Ayatullah Sayyid Ali al-Husseini al-Sistani
- ❖ Shia Muslims: Our Identity, Our Vision, and the Way Forward by Sayyid M.B. Kashmiri
- ❖ Who is Hussain? by Dr. Mehdi Saeed Hazari
  Also available in Spanish
- ❖ The Illuminating Lantern: An Exposition of Subtleties from the Quran by Shaykh Habib al-Kadhimi
- ❖ Tajwid: A Guide to Quranic Recitation by Shaykh Rizwan Arastu
- ❖ God's Emissaries: Adam to Jesus by Shaykh Rizwan Arastu
- ❖ Fasting: A Haven from Hellfire by Grand Ayatullah Sayyid Ali al-Husseini al-Sistani